WRITING PAST DARK

WRITING PAST DARK

Envy, Fear, Distraction, and Other Dilemmas in the Writer's Life

Bonnie Friedman

HarperPerennial
A Division of HarperCollins*Publishers*

For my parents,
Lawrence and Elise Friedman

Grateful acknowledgment is made to the New York Times Company for permission to reprint "Envy, the Writer's Disease." From the *New York Times Book Review*. Copyright November 26, 1989, by the New York Times Company. Reprinted by permission.

Mountain Tasting: Zen Haiku by Santōka Taneda. Translated and introduced by John Stevens, John Weatherhill Inc., 1980.

A hardcover edition of this book was published in 1993 by HarperCollins Publishers.

HarperCollins books may be purchased for educational, business, or sales promotional use. For information please write Special Markets Department, HarperCollins Publishers, Inc., 10 East 53rd Street, New York, NY 10022.

First HarperPerennial edition published 1994.

Designed by C. Linda Dingler

The Library of Congress has catalogued the hardcover edition as follows:
Friedman, Bonnie
   Writing past dark : envy, fear, distraction, and other dilemmas in the writer's life / Bonnie Friedman.—1st ed.
   p. cm.
   ISBN 0-06-016607-X
   1. Authorship—Psychological aspects. 2. Authors—Psychology.
3. Creation (Literary, artistic, etc.) 4. Emotions. I. Title.
PN171.P83F75   1993
808' .02' 019—dc20   92-54732

ISBN 0-06-092200-1 (pbk.)

95 96 97 98 ❖/RRD H 10 9 8 7 6

One does not become enlightened by imagining figures of light,
but by making the darkness conscious.
—Carl Jung

Wet with morning dew,
I go in the direction I want.
—Santōka Taneda

Contents

Acknowledgments

MY DEEP THANKS TO ALETHEA YOUNG, who returned my words to me the year I lost them.

I am grateful to many friends: Gary Glickman gave me constant inspiration, an espresso pot, and a Tunisian candlestick. Priscilla Sneff and Peggy Merrill always found something valuable in my pages. Karen Venezia built me a room to write in when every footfall upstairs made me leap. Elizabeth Evans, Kathie Min, Martha Ramsey, Erica Funkhauser, and Carole Slipowitz read a draft of this book and offered helpful suggestions. John Kane taught me how to look into a lens. And my sister Anita constantly provided an extraordinary example of grace under pressure.

I am also grateful to the MacDowell Colony for giving me a month of heaven; to Malaga Baldi, my agent, who championed this book when it scarcely existed; and to Cynthia Barrett, my editor, whose know-how was essential to completing it.

And thanks most especially to Paul, who sustained me with love and fishes.

Why I Wrote This Book

THE HAPPIEST I'VE EVER BEEN was departing before dawn to the bus station in Madrid. The tiny bread shop and the tobacconist were still dark. The wet pavement gleamed when a city bus heaved past. Ahead of me lay unknown towns and countrysides that matched names I knew only from a map, and a new friend who was herself departing just then from across Madrid clutching a plastic bag like mine that was filled, like mine, with an egg-and-potato sandwich and a tangerine. The world was doors opening in all directions. I felt free, and awake, and full of laughter.

Writing has often been just like that for me. Sometimes though this life is hard, and not because of how tricky it is to invent convincing dialogue or because I need to decide whether the one story I'm telling really ought to be two. It is hard because there is no friend departing from the opposite direction who I can anticipate meeting me in the middle. It is hard because it is done alone.

This "alone" has many aspects to it. Of course we have to think up our words in the solitude of our own minds. But we are also alone because lots of the difficulties we face we don't give voice to. Envy, that corrosive, itchy emotion, stalks us in the pages of the daily newspaper, the picture of a young famous author like a hole we can fall through. How to save ourselves? And the urge to write a certain story, but the knowledge it would hurt the person it was about—what to do? And what about the lure of apprenticeship, the mystique of the mentor, the fear of writing something embarrassing and wasting a lot of time at it, the fear of silence itself, and the suspicion that perhaps, after all, one is in fact deluded, unspecial, unmagical, that the map one is departing into will never bloom on the page into real almond blossoms and tumbling blue rivers and dank cathedrals?

The first book I ever owned was a pop-up book. Mr. and Mrs. Crayon drove their orange box through city streets. When I pulled the heavy page from right to left, apartment buildings rose, and zoo cages leapt with tigers, and ladies pushed baby carriages. That book taught me what writing ought to be. But how do we know if our imaginations contain lofting landscapes? What about the days when everything inside feels flat, flat, a mouth gone sour, a winter sky like a tomb, every word cliché? What about the days when words shrink what we mean, make it dollhouse furniture, a parody, something we can't stand?

I wanted a book that would be a companion I could reach for. The bookstore shelves sagged with volumes on technique. A hundred authors explained how to show don't tell, and why a story needs a conflict. Why hadn't anyone written the book that would help me? I dreamed of a book like a friend also traveling through the night, a friend with a compass, and secrets to share about her own experience. How much better I always felt after talking with a writer friend!

One day, because I had discovered so much about envy over the years, I decided to write down what I knew. When that essay was printed, many people wrote to me to let me know what a relief it was to have this subject addressed, and to tell their own story. But there were so many other parts of the writer's life that were equally undiscussed and rich! I decided to write for others the book I wished someone had written for me. It was exciting, and filled me with energy to look at the emotional side of the writer's life.

In every writing class I've been in there was a brilliant student, a student whose words flung out in morning glories and birds-of-paradise on the page, and who left the rest of us gaping when he or she was done reading, inspired and even thankful. Almost every single one of those writers has disappeared! Devoured by the world, or by their own psyches. Devoured perhaps by their resolute blindness to their own beauty.

Successful writers are not the ones who write the best sentences. They are the ones who keep writing. They are the ones who discover what is most important and strangest and most pleasurable in themselves, and keep believing in the value of their work, despite the difficulties.

This book is meant to keep you going despite the difficulties. In fact, it looks inside the difficulties to see the messages hidden in there, like messages scrolled into your dreams, so powerful and alluring. We are constantly telling ourselves what we most want to know, and at the same time are deaf to it. Why does envy have such a fierce bite? Why do we fall silent or get worried just as our story is about to spring out of our control and into its own life? Whose shadow falls across the page?

When my friend met me in the Madrid bus station dawn was just then lighting the streets. She asked the ticket vendor, "Where do you suggest we go for a good day trip?"

"Why don't you try Cercanías?" the woman said.

Cercanías! What a mellifluous town it sounded like it would be! It sounded ringed by a river, babbling, coursing, full of music.

"Yes! Give us tickets!" we cried, pushing our money toward her.

She laughed. Cercanías merely means nearby places, as opposed to Lejanías, which is everything far away.

My friend and I studied the sign marked Cercanías and boarded the very next bus to the first place on the list. We set off to what is exotic and nearby. This book is a similar journey. Looking at the emotional side of the writer's life freed me. I hope it does the same for you.

ENVY, THE
WRITER'S DISEASE

I T USED TO BE LIKE A FEVER WITH ME, a compulsion, a madness:
to go into a bookstore, head straight for the brand-new books,
flip right to the back of the jacket and see if the author was
young or old, my age or even—rats!—younger. Envy is a voca-
tional hazard for most writers. It festers in one's mind, distracting
one from one's own work, at its most virulent even capable of
rousing the sufferer from sleep to brood over another's triumph.

Envy is the green-eyed beast. It is a sickness; it is a hunger. It
is the self consuming the self. It takes what was most beloved—
reading books, writing them—and sours it, a quick drop of vine-
gar into the glass of sweet milk. Even friendships aren't exempt.
"That story of mine?" your friend says at lunch. "*The New Yorker*
took it. I thought you knew."

A finger has tapped your heart. You smile. This is your friend.
Surely you feel happy for your friend. And yet a space opens
between you. You can feel it there, wide enough for a cool breeze
to blow across.

What is this thing that can take the best from us and yet
remain unsatisfied? When I think of envy, I think of Pharaoh's
lean cows. They eat up the healthy ones—cannibals, those
cows!—yet they remain as skinny as ever, so that, the Bible tells
us, "when they had eaten them up, it could not be known that
they had eaten them; but they were still ill favored, as at the

beginning." I've always felt sorry for those cows. We're told they're poor and lean-fleshed, emaciated and ugly. They feed, but cannot digest. They are unhealthy desire incarnate.

Another image of envy—this time not of my conjecturing, but called Envy by its author—comes from an anonymous late medieval poet:

> Where Envy rokketh in the corner yond,
> And sitteth dirk; and ye shall see anone
> His lenë bodie, fading face and hond;
> Him-self he fretteth, as I understond.

Envy sits in the corner, hidden, hiding, starved. His face and hand are fading, so thin is he, so insubstantial has he become from fretting himself. ("To fret" here meant to gnaw away at or to rub away. A medieval cookbook directed one to fret an apple through a sieve. "Fret" also refers, of course, to an agitation of the mind, a vexation.)

Envy frets himself. He is alone, his own victim. He is self-absorbed. He is self-propelled. It does not take two to envy. Somehow it takes only one.

Cynthia Ozick, that miracle word-spinner, speaks of envy in a generous interview published in *Writers at Work: The Paris Review Interviews, Eighth Series*. "Youth," she says, "is for running around in the great world, not for sitting in a hollow cell, turning into an unnatural writing-beast. There one sits, reading and writing, month after month, year after year. There one sits, envying other young writers who have achieved a grain more than oneself. Without the rush and brush and crush of the world, one becomes hollowed out. The cavity fills with envy. A wasting disease that takes years and years to recover from."

What is this thing that has us chewing at our own selves, grating ourselves against our own sharp sieve? It is the act of stepping back. It is the act of separating, and judging. It takes only one because the one becomes two. The self separates from the self. It points a finger and declares, "You are good" or "You are bad." Either one, it doesn't matter. The first statement usually flips over to become the second. And vice versa. Either way, the separated self is not *doing* the writing. Envious, the self is *thinking* about the writing, *thinking* about the self, rocking in its dark corner.

The self steps back and pretends to be the world. It says: "I too think that self is ugly. I too condemn it." If you condemn it, you cannot be it. Thus the envious self protects itself from feeling puny. It identifies with the powerful, with the world that may condemn the self. It is not the inferior one—far from it! It will take that inferior one and punish it against that sieve. Envy fretteth him-self.

That sharp sieve may be a favorable review of someone else's book. It may be the book in our hand, showing the author's glowing face. What is she? Fifteen? There are a million sieves in the world, many in the shape of a book—that thing we loved most, transformed.

Even Shakespeare was tormented by this transformation: "When in disgrace with fortune and men's eyes / . . . Desiring this man's art, and that man's scope." *Shakespeare* desired another's art? Dear Lord, whose? And doesn't this prove that envy is one of the scorpions of the mind, often having little to do with the objective, external world? "With what I most enjoy contented least," the poet says. "Yet in these thoughts myself almost despising." For Shakespeare too, apparently, the source of pleasure could be transformed into a painful sieve. Even he could end up with a sense of almost self-loathing.

Perhaps an elemental sense of being neglected *precedes* the adult experience of recognition or neglect. I'm not saying that many people don't have just cause to feel slighted, to feel jealous of another's gifts. I'm suggesting that the sense of being deprived may preexist mature experience. So that as adults, we are often reminded of that earlier state. So that we are more attuned to repetitions of that same experience of hunger, and we may even transform neutral experiences into ones in which we can recon-firm our own earlier state. Perhaps some of us even go so far as to become deaf to positive experiences or to find some way to dis-credit them.

I had a friend at writing school who won many prizes and got enthusiastic letters from editors. But whenever I went to visit her, she said, "Look at this letter! Another rejection—I'm so depressed!" It's true it was another rejection, but what about the wild praise that preceded the "Please send more work," the great big dollops of heavy cream? I'd sit on the couch, sick at heart that the letter wasn't mine, while my friend scanned my face. Did my misery really prove to her that her work was loved? Could she really nourish herself from my face? Strindberg writes about ego vampires, and I suppose my friend, in a way, was one. Still, I can't believe the sustenance she derived from my unhap-piness stayed with her. She showed the letter to the next person who visited, and the one after that. She ate, but starved. The no in the letter drowned out all the yes.

"I want to be a star," this woman once told me, unabashed. We were walking through a heavy, swinging door, and I stopped a moment, stunned, before I pushed through. What awed me was not that she wanted to be a star—didn't we all?—but that she'd say so, flat out. I thought if you had the gumption to say what you wanted, you'd probably have the nerve to get it. And I was, in fact, impressed by her desire. Most of us wanted the same thing, but we tried not to know it. Such grand wants exact a price. Better to content oneself with the small success.

"I am ashamed to confess this," Cynthia Ozick says in her *Paris Review* interview. "It's ungrateful and wrong. But I am one—how full of shame I feel as I confess this—who expected to achieve—can I dare get this out of my throat?—something like—impossible to say the words—Literary Fame by the age of twenty-five. By the age of twenty-seven I saw that Holy and Anointed Youth was over, and even then it was already too late."

Too late! We will either be Thomas Mann or nobody. We

will be F. Scott Fitzgerald or we ought not to exist at all. And some young writers actually do make it. Look, there's Susan Minot, there's David Leavitt and Michael Chabon. Names on the pages, photos in the magazines, as if to prove it can still be done, real achievement and fame in one fell swoop in the flush of what Ozick calls "Anointed Youth."

In an episode of the old television comedy "Car 54, Where Are You?" Officer Gunther Toody tries to reassure his partner, Francis Muldoon, who is grieving because his father made police captain when he was years younger than Francis is now. "Don't feel bad," Gunther says. "People were younger back then." I've believed that! People *were* younger back then. But then I open some journal or magazine and see that people are just as young today.

It's desire that causes envy. Isn't desire the villain here? Yet how to be an artist without desire? How far would you get? Without desire, could you send a story out again and again, after it's been rejected? Without desire, could you sit back down at the desk after some friend has enlightened you so thoroughly about your poor little story that now its flaws loom like the gaping pores and massive nostrils of the Brobdingnagians? The piece appalls you, but you go on. You tape the rejection notice to the fridge and send the story out again. Desire spurs you and sustains you. And yet it does you in.

Melanie Klein, that controversial and pioneering post-Freudian, says that envy starts in infancy. In the essay "A Study of Envy and Gratitude," she says, "The first object to be envied is the feeding breast, for the infant feels that it possesses everything that he desires and that it has an unlimited flow of milk and love which it keeps for its own gratification." The baby is frustrated because he cannot gratify himself. It is the mother who has the power here, the mother who determines whether he feels hungry or sated, miserable or safe. Envy, Klein says, is "bound up with . . . projection." The infant imagines that the breast, which inevitably frustrates him, which at some point or another is at least briefly absent, hoards its pleasures for itself. In response, the infant feels anger and greed. "Greed is an impetuous and insatiable craving," Klein writes. "At the unconscious level, greed aims primarily at completely scooping out, sucking dry and devouring the breast . . . whereas envy not only aims at robbing in this way, but also at putting badness . . . into the mother . . . It is the nature of envy that it spoils the primal good object." Enraged by his utter dependence, the infant tries to ruin what he most loved.

Projection is at the core of envy. As adults, we may project onto others—editors, other writers—a great awareness of what we imagine to be our own disempowerment. We may project onto others the possession of a perfect, delightful, hoarded life. We may project the power ultimately to judge our talent. We may project the power to decide if we should be happy or not, whether we should accept or reject our own work—even, perhaps, whether we should accept or reject our own selves.

Of course, if you're going to give that much power away, you're going to resent like hell whomever you give it to. Envy has projection at its core. One becomes two: you give away part of yourself, then feel lean and hungry, and you long for what you've given away. If praise comes, it satisfies only briefly. How could it be otherwise? The praise comes from outside you; the prize is given by a man or woman who is not you. You long for something—a sign, an unequivocal sign—that you are a good writer, that what you write is worthwhile. Signs come, sometimes many, sometimes few. But how can there be enough? Like Pharaoh's cows, we eat and starve. What one longs to take into oneself is what one has given away: the power to say yes.

"I just sent my manuscript to an agent," a friend once told me. "I hope he holds on to it for a long, long time. I really want to get some writing done, and know if he sends it back I'll be too depressed to do anything. If he rejects it, I'll be in a slump." She gazed at me, miserable.

"Have you considered sending it to a second agent if it comes back?" I asked. The thought hadn't occurred to her. She had this one man's name—a stranger, someone whose tastes she didn't know, simply a name on a page—and off she sent her fate.

"Why do we seek fame?" a student asks the spiritual teacher Krishnamurti, according to a book entitled *Think on These Things*.

"Have you ever thought about it?" he responds. "We want to be famous as a writer, as a poet, as a painter, as a politician, as a singer, or what you will. Why? Because we really don't love what we are doing. If you loved to sing, or to paint, or to write poems—if you really loved it—you would not be concerned with whether you are famous or not ... Our present education is rotten because it teaches us to love success and not what we are doing. The result has become more important than the action.

"You know," he continues, "it is good to hide your brilliance under a bushel, to be anonymous, to love what you are doing and not to show off. It is good to be kind without a name. That does not make you famous, it does not cause your photograph to appear in the newspapers. Politicians do not come to your door. You are just a creative human being living anonymously, and in that there is richness and great beauty."

Just one thing saves me from envy: returning to my work. My desk is a quiet place. My hours there are like panes of clear glass. Empty, composed, they are ready to hold any image. I sit down and try to hear my characters. What is Louise saying today? What is happening with sweet, troubled Anna? Theirs is a separate world that I must write my way into. Theirs is a separate world that waits while I rush about, fixing meals, making beds, getting jealous and unjealous and maybe jealous again.

What do they care? When I am at my desk, when I'm receptive, they'll speak. When I'm in the midst of their world, there is only them, and what they do and say and think. Anna is putting on weight, poor dear, and her mother is enforcing a diet. Louise is reading dirty magazines in the drugstore after school and is afraid that someone will find out. And Stuey is absorbed with his fish tank; he has firemouth cichlids, cardinal tetras, glass catfish with skeletons that you can see clear through their bodies. But the sound of the water pump is driving Martin mad! He gets up in the middle of the night. He grabs the fish tank with both hands and hoists it in his arms. But water—how could he forget how heavy water is? He lugs the thing three steps and then—and then I don't exist. I am gone. What exists is only the writing. And when the writing goes well, its pleasure lasts the whole day. It is the writing that saves you, not your own self.

"One *must* avoid ambition *in order to* write," Ozick says. "Otherwise something else is the goal: some kind of power beyond the power of language. And the power of language, it seems to me, is the only kind of power a writer is entitled to . . . [These days] I think *only* of what it is I want to write about, and then about the problems in the doing of it. I don't think of anything else at all."

Envy is a con man, a tugger at your sleeve, a knocker at your door. Let me in for just a moment, it says, for just one moment of your time. It claims to tell the truth; it craves attention. The more you listen to it, the more you believe what it says. The more thoroughly you believe, the more you think you must listen. You must get the info on who is out there, how young the competition is, where they've been reviewed, what they've won, and what that means about you. The antidote to envy is one's own work. Always one's own work. Not the thinking about it. Not the assessing of it. But the *doing* of it. The answers you want can come only from the work itself. It drives the spooks away.

MESSAGE FROM A CLOUD OF FLIES: ON DISTRACTION

I SPENT THIS MORNING SMASHING FLIES. I meant to be writing my novel. In fact, I'd already read over a few pages of it to hear the narrator's voice again, and copied onto a fresh piece of unlined yellow paper the last sentences from yesterday, and I was just about to come up with something new—when my ears buzzed. On the glass before me hung the black thick body of a fly. I decided to get rid of it so I could concentrate.

I rolled up a section of *The Globe* and returned to the desk. The fly remained in the exact same spot, as if glued. I swung, struck, thought, There, that's done—but when I lifted the baton: nothing. The fly hovered so close my bare arm tickled. Then it swooped to another window. I slammed—a direct hit!—but at that very instant two more flies sprang off the glass as if popped into the universe. I was surprised: all our windows have screens. This was a humid, hot day, though, the last sigh of summer after two crisp weeks, and perhaps that had drawn them.

I killed one fly against the doorjamb. Another I stalked into the kitchen and got against the fridge. A third fly wavered by the kitchen window. When I swatted, a wild ferocious swing, a whole trembling crowd shot from the window like pebbles from a blunderbuss, then settled back.

My heart pounded. I felt flushed with disgust and irritation. Why must I always have such obstacles to my writing? I craved to be submerged, to be "into" my novel, to be in that state when words come fast, and the characters walk and talk the way characters in your dreams do—without your conscious desire. It is like snorkeling: you go under, and there is a whole secret life. You go under, and scarlet fish shimmer past, fluttering like silk, watched perhaps by a gaping blue-striped grunt with a yellow eye, or there's a barracuda, all set to lunge. Outside, you saw just the water's surface mirroring back your own choppy face and the familiar, corrugated world. Submerged, breathing through a tube, you have a strange freedom from gravity, and an awareness of beauty like a bodily hum.

I craved that world, not this. I longed to go under. So frequently, though, there were obstacles: a bag of Growth Iambs my cat needed, an oil leak in the Civic (the landlady left a surly message about it on my answering machine), an insurance form I had to fill out and send to Minneapolis regarding last month's strep throat.

So many flies! I killed one against the window frame. Another buzzed against the glass as if it hoped to drown in it, and, when I swung, the breeze split the one in two and then I killed them both. I killed five, six, seven flies—I was furious! The more I wanted to end them, though, the more I had to study them, and they repulsed me more and more—the plump iridescent bluish bodies, the shifting plates, the gigantic reddish heads above the fragile legs. Once I struck the glass so hard it cracked. I sat down once, composed my mind, picked up my pen, and just as I was about to start writing saw a fly's wings and blood clinging to my hand. Another time I sat down, wrote two sentences, and heard—could it be?—a faint buzz, then the thud as a small body hit glass.

I would not learn. I was a human being controlled by a fly. Education, discipline, artistic vision—gone. My eyes were mesmerized and my arms followed scrupulously the movements of an insect. It ruled me. I let it. I wanted to get everything in that room just right before my writing began. I was afraid that just as a good idea was about to come to me, about to leap the synapse and appear full-blown, a fly would appear, and jar me, and the idea would fall in the gap and be lost forever, something impossible to recall because it was never really *known*.

It was my very commitment to writing that kept me from it. I wanted so much for it to be that ideal, submerged experience that I put it off. I saved it up. I longed for it, missed it, got bitchy about it, petulant, then again thought of it with a pang—an adored but long-gone love. What if the cherished one really isn't so beautiful after all? What if he turns out to be, upon reunion, slow, dumb, greedy, with lips that are thin and colorless—not at all as you'd remembered!

You love your work, so you don't touch it. You love your writing, so it's the very thing you must not do at all. You could not tolerate it if it didn't come out well. You could not tolerate yourself. You are thinking about the work, thinking about yourself, looking at the surface of the water, looking at the choppy face looking back.

"To distract" originally meant to rend into parts. It's from the Latin for "to draw in different directions, to pull asunder," and calls to mind the ancient torture of roping a man to horses and having them charge off in opposite directions. Distraction wrenches apart; it scatters and divides. The word also meant, as it does now, to draw someone from his or her actual destination, to perplex, and to derange in mind.

Those flies divided me up in a dozen tangled ways. Part of me craved my writing, part of me craved killing flies, part of me saw myself killing flies and said this makes no sense, and part said this *makes* sense, and part of me was aware of myself looking at myself like looking down a hall of mirrors. Eyes complex as an insect's stared back. An insect has compound eyes, each eye an array of facets, a crowded honeycomb of lenses. Images splinter in, the world a prism place, full of distraction.

Distraction said to me, I am the true path. I am the way to your beloved destination. Follow me and soon you'll be able to undistractedly write. I am the way to Concentration, Distraction said. It spoke in the voice of logic. It always took as its subject just this one last fly. It consumed tremendous energy. I whirled like a dervish, in place. I flapped like a human with an ant mask on. My cheeks were flushed with it, my head buzzed with it—the more distracted I was, the more distracted I became. The more I wanted cleanliness, the more my hands were smeared with filth. The more I yearned to be into my writing, the more I was decisively out.

On the Jewish New Year there is a prayer: "On New Year's Day the decree is inscribed and on the Day of Atonement it is sealed . . . who shall have rest and who go wandering; who shall be tranquil and who shall be disturbed; who shall be at ease and who shall be afflicted."

When I was a girl, I wondered at this prayer. I thought it was no curse to go wandering. All the best people were off wandering in those days, in painted vans, or hitching rides by the roadside. Almost all eventually settled somewhere or other. It is the curse of the pariah, of Cain himself, to be "a ceaseless wanderer." Unknown and unknowing, it is a living death. One can follow any road. Any road's just as good. Up every lane pipes a voice: "Follow me!"

I am drawn into distraction because I want to be distracted. It is a common choice. Compare the number of people who are "blocked" with the number who actually write, and you'd probably find a vast, shadow people, a ghostly populace caught within the lack of words. "Just do it," is the frequent advice, like a Nike ad. When I heard the tiny thud of yet another fly landing on the window, though, I rose from the desk. I knew about the sticky, seductive nature of distraction, yet I chose it.

I thought, If I can't control this room, how can I control my writing? Yet the essence of writing is not control, but release. Plan your story's path too narrowly, blinder it like a hack horse lugging a bunch of characters up the street—no, you may not go down that alley; no, to you that road must be a painted backdrop—and the damn thing balks. The story won't budge. Or else it shatters in tiny pieces, like a pencil ground too sharp, pressed too hard. Graphite clutters the page, and the point just lies there, an amputated thing.

When writing is going well it is not like pushing. It's like falling. You fall the way you do in dreams. You fall and fall. There is that same disorientation and breathlessness and speed and tension. You fall past the ground floor, past the sub-basement, past the creatures that live in the center of the earth, big black lobsterlike figures working machines you glimpse as you fall toward blue sky. What joy! And yet, it's scary. For all its vast pleasure, it's scary because falling stops, words end, and it is always just you again at your desk in your room, judgment already beginning.

We have an aversion to loss of control, as much as we love it. We have an almost instinctive revulsion to people and things that are out of control or whom reason doesn't rule: drunk people, rioting people, the snake suddenly underfoot, the cockroach in the kitchen, unbridled nature, big as death. American history is an onslaught against wildness. All that chopping and burning and shooting at Indians reveal men appalled by what seemed untamed. We are terrified as much as we are enthralled by what seems wild, and by our own wildness. We don't know what will come out of it. We don't know what will come out of us. Perhaps something good. Perhaps ugly things, awful sentiments, perhaps hideous crawling bugs. We may awake in our writing to find ourselves Gregor Samsa.

I killed the bugs outside me because I longed to kill the bugs inside. I was afraid, I've said, that just as a good idea was about to come to me, a fly would appear. I was afraid the good idea would *be* a fly, an ugly appalling thing, something I wished would disappear.

Yet the things that disgust also fascinate. We don't want to look, but our eyes dart over. We sleep and they loom in our dreams. En masse we gaze at what we dare not see alone: bodies decomposing, you can see the worms; a mummy-faced creature with fingers that are knives; a machine that murders and murders—there's no stopping it, it's crushed but repairs itself, always ending up gleaming like new. Horror films, bloody movies—we laugh, but go. It's a thrill. Or we don't go but the images reach us anyway. In dreams, we are locked together. The night is dark, the body paralyzed with sleep. One is helpless before one's own thoughts. They arise and arise, although you prohibit them. They are impervious as the Martians in *War of the Worlds*. We don't know how to make them stop. One last defense works for a while. Dawn comes, and we wake to forget.

"It often happens," Freud notes, "that the account first given of a dream is incomplete and that the memory of the omitted portions only emerges in the course of analysis . . . a part of a dream that has been rescued from oblivion in this way is invariably the most important part."

Freud likens the nonjudgmental mood necessary for remembering dreams to the attitude needed to write creatively: "The adoption of the required attitude of mind towards ideas that seem to emerge 'of their own free will' and the abandonment of the critical function that is normally in operation against them seem to be hard of achievement for some people. The 'involuntary thoughts' are liable to release a most violent resistance, which seeks to prevent their emergence. If we may trust that great poet and philosopher Friedrich von Schiller, however, poetic creation must demand an exactly similar attitude."

My resistance this morning was certainly "violent." I waged a furious attack. I acted out the role of censor, annihilating the unbidden with my paper bat. Freud calls the peculiarities of dreams "repugnant" to waking thought. He describes their "transitory character, the manner in which waking thought pushes them on one side, as something alien to it, and mutilates or extinguishes them in memory." All that disgust this morning—from what instinct did it spring?

We want to abandon ourselves in our writing, to experience images that come to us "of their own free will," and yet we are opposed to it. We are, in fact, ambivalent. Ambivalence, Harold Bloom reminds us, was used by Freud to mean "a simultaneous love and hatred directed toward the same object."

Writer's "block" embodies this ambivalence. One calls oneself a writer, but one who is "blocked." The block obstructs the passageway. It is a thing lodged in the throat, prohibiting speech. It is a boulder jammed in the mouth of the cave. The repressed cannot exit. The buried is kept below. Of course we know the repressed *will* out—but if you have a good solid block, at least it won't disgorge itself all over the unequivocal page. The block is like a man's Adam's apple, a sign of sin, of one's own suspected sin, stuck almost painfully in one's throat.

Not-writing has the same source as writing. It is the secret sharer. It is the yin of writing's yang. It is the tapeworm in the belly, the parasite that feeds at the host's expense, debilitating, hard to see, potent and obscure. It consumes the words one would have said. It hides them in itself, able to absorb as intensely as a black hole, collapsing entire worlds inside it and remaining dark as before. "Tap into what you don't want to say," urges movie director Arthur Penn. "Tap into that secret place, despite the agony, despite the personal pain, over and above the fatigue. This one little piece of me I want to get down on film."

This is the piece that craves words *and* silence.

We are afraid of writing, even those of us who love it. And there are parts of it we hate. The necessary mess, the loss of control, its ability to betray us, as well as the possibility that what we write might be lousy, it might just stink (it might just stink and we'll know it's ours, or worse, we might think it's lovely and show it to others only to realize by their constrained, uncomfortable response, that in fact we let loose a bad one)—how to feel at ease with all this? How just to let one's work be?

Our horror of the spontaneous emission and our obsession with perfection make us mute. We want beauty so badly we're speechless. We want the face of Dorian Gray: perfect no matter what. Never mind the poor soul was driven to ever greater corruption, provoked by his beautiful, impervious face. We want it. And what terrifies is the possibility that instead we'll end up with his cracked, decaying portrait, the pustules, the leer. Keep it in the closet! Lock it up and throw away the key!

But no, we keep the key in a deep vest pocket. We hide it on ourselves. We finger it from time to time. There it is: the key. It is a small, solid thing, like a stump of pencil. It takes up a definite space. Hard to believe so small a thing could hold such power. You toss it in the air while strolling. You slip it in your pants, jangle it against your change. It is a secret you keep with yourself—a little private joke. But oh, if it should fall into the wrong hands! So you keep it, and when you change your pants or your vest, your shirt or your shoes, you don't for a minute forget where it is. Afraid of losing it, you want it lost. It weighs a ton, it weighs nothing at all. What is it? Give up? If only you could! Give up, and the answer appears. Give up, and you are released. Give up, give up—let the bells toll it throughout your land. Struggle, and clarity of mind disperses. Surrender, and somehow it's yours.

The quality of concentration is not strained. "It droppeth as the gentle rain of heaven / Upon the place below." A writer's concentration is not only like mercy, it is mercy, mercy toward oneself. It is allowing imperfection. It is allowing mess. Even what stinks must be allowed into one's heaven. Even what has been considered paltry, contemptible, must have its place. Bar the lowly, and no one worthwhile will enter. Accept, and a teeming crowd appears, a whole mixed multitude of beggars and billionaires, quiet louts and loudmouth saints. The mutter, the cracked voice, the false start, the false start again, all precede the song. Those who write do have a trick. They lean on the process of writing the way an unsteady person leans on a cane. Not by sheer genius alone does the work advance. Not by an inchoate blaze from the head.

If you have few expectations for a piece, if you don't load it up with the baggage of the ego like an immigrant cart strapped with every single pot and pillow to be carried into the new life, surprisingly, the story or poem often gets good. That's the tricky part, not letting its goodness get in your way. Not being afraid to touch the half-finished piece for fear of messing it up. Letting yourself surrender your hopes for it again and again.

In New York I saw a Buddhist monk making a sand mandala. He had six or seven bowls of colored sand—egg-yolk orange, midnight blue, dusty gray among them—and a metal cone the size of a bull's horn, which had a tiny hole at the end. The monk scooped a bit of sand into the cone, and when he tapped, a trickle of sand beaded out of the hole a few grains at a time. With this he painted elaborate, complicated scenes: a procession of elephants looped tail to trunk, many-tiered palaces, flying birds, regal tigers, each intricate quarter of the design mirroring the opposite quarter in byzantine symmetry, the entire disk perhaps four feet across. In the hour I watched—this was in the Museum of Natural History, at the raging height of an apocalyptically hot summer—the monk shaped the tail of a lion. First he used yellow. Then he shaded with an echoing curve of red, then white. The tail shimmered like a flame.

It was a meditation to construct this mandala. It was being drawn for the spiritual benefit of the artist and of those people who would see it. The monk leaned intently over his trickle of sand. It would take three months to finish the work. It would take hundreds of hours of steady focus. Then, when it was done—kaput! He'd throw it to the wind. Or he would take it and toss it into the sea "for," a sign explained, "the spiritual benefit of the fish."

That is how it is with sand mandalas. With them, it's all in the doing. When they're done, they're gone. How can he bear it? I thought. In every tap of the funnel there is farewell. In every movement of the wrist, good-bye, good-bye. The reward for the effort is giving it to the wind, giving it to the fish in the sea, doing it to be doing it, not to have it done.

Oh, to write openhandedly! To do it letting go! I've wanted that and wanted that, and sometimes it's just come to me like the gentle rain of heaven, but more often I've received it after practice, after much practice managing to outdistance even my acquisitive self.

I knew a man who believed a bee had been sent to earth to give him a message. He was sitting on a hilltop in Mexico, after smoking peyote. A bee hovered near him. It hovered and did not depart. It stayed so long he began to think it had a reason to be with him. It had chosen him, he thought. It was a spirit, a soul, a familiar. It brought a message of blessing and peace. It reassured him, sitting there.

A few days later this man found out his mother was dying in New York. He returned to that city and stayed in a room in a rent-by-the-week hotel in Chelsea while she slowly died. His room was cold and shabby and gave onto an airshaft. He was either at the hospital or he was there. He remembered that bee at that time. Years later he still remembered it.

If a bee in Mexico can bring a message, then a fly in Massachusetts can, too. My fly says, "Let me hover near you. Kill me and kill me, and I will come back. You will exhaust yourself in useless struggle. Let me be, and soon you will forget I'm here." Accept the fly before you, accept the fly that appears on the page. Who knows? You may even come to find beauty in its strange company.

YOUR MOTHER'S PASSIONS, YOUR SISTER'S WOES: WRITING ABOUT THE LIVING

───────────

For centuries Dedalus has represented the type of the artist-scientist: that curiously disinterested, almost diabolic human phenomenon, beyond the normal bounds of social judgment, dedicated to the morals not of his time but of his art.

—JOSEPH CAMPBELL

THE BEST STORIES I KNOW I MUST NOT TELL. One of them concerns my cousin Robert. I haven't seen him in years. As children we went to the same bungalow colony, and amid the Creamsicle and lemon summer houses and oceans of hot, clipped grass, there was simply the sense that there was something strange about Robert (this is not his real name).

He was, I think, prone to frantic, unappeasable tantrums when he should have been too old for them, and he wandered into the girls' changing room with his pants unzipped, so that now the smell of frilled rubber bathing caps and mildewed carpeting always calls to mind for me that ribbon of pink flesh, a bald human bookmark soon squashed and hidden—but not before Robert absorbed our horror, his big eyes staring.

My mother remembers him earlier, as a very little boy strolling down to the lake in Mount Liberty, fat, with a yeasty white belly and bare feet, a red sand pail overturned on his head.

"He looked so funny," my mother says, "with that bucket down over his head."

"Maybe he was pretending to be a soldier, and the bucket was his helmet."

"No-o," she says, pondering. "I don't think it was that. The bucket was too low for that. It was right down over his face."

And now recently a different cousin, Charlotte, ran into Robert. They had a long talk. He is a nice-looking young man with dark hair, and he is no longer fat. "He told me," she says, "that it sometimes takes four or five hours to leave the house. He will look in the mirror and see something about his appearance that bothers him, and he will have to change it. He washes his hair over and over so he can blow-dry it correctly. He buttons and unbuttons the top button of his shirt."

"Five hours?" I say. "That's an exaggeration."

"No, I don't think so. If you met him, I'm sure you'd think it was true."

She can't tell me anything else about him, though, because in fact he swore her to silence.

"Oh, come on," I say.

She shakes her head. "I shouldn't have told you this much. Still, if you'd met him—there is just something so odd about him . . . "

Robert lives on disability at an undisclosed address in Ocean City—he won't tell his parents where. If I described his brittle, caustic mother, his jumpy brother, his reclusive father, you could probably see how all their lives have been shaped by Robert, and how his life has been shaped by theirs.

This man's life, everything about him, is the family secret. And I want to write about it.

Similarly, I'd like to write about the woman who lived down the hall from us in apartment 5B when I was growing up. Her parents forbade her to marry the man she loved because he wasn't a Jew.

"What was he?" I asked.

"He was in fact a very religious man. Kept kosher, kept his head covered." My mother shrugged. "He *was* Jewish, but for Mrs. Landau nobody was good enough. She told Stella if she married him, forget it. She wouldn't have anything to do with her."

Stella broke off the engagement and took a long trip around the world, but had to come home early because she'd contracted a disease. One of the symptoms of this disease was that she could not walk. Another was that her stomach was so weak she could hardly eat. She lay down in her parents' apartment, and her mother nursed her for month after month.

I was in that apartment. It was in those days a murky place with two tiny bedrooms that funneled into a kitchenette. A dog we called "the pickle dog" because of its yellow-green fur seemed to decompose on the linoleum. The father, a man with a stiff broad upper body like a door, sat at the table mutely reading a newspaper. The mother, in lumpy dark wool clothes she'd sewn herself, clothes so thick it seemed a whole box of pins could disappear inside, stirred the pot of saltless spinach soup that always simmered, releasing a pervasive vegetable scent. And Stella drowsed in one of the bedrooms, letting herself be nursed.

Of course she was brought from doctor to doctor as the seasons passed. A fortune was spent. Her tests all turned up normal. At last it was decided she must have been infected by a rare tropical virus no American doctor could recognize. Around this time Stella got up, recovered her health, and married the man she loved. Her mother, true to her word, wouldn't see her. She hung up when the daughter phoned. In the elevator she merely blinked, one long stony blink, if a neighbor asked about Stella. At last, after three years, the mother admitted defeat, and took

the train to Mount Kisco to visit the grandson whose face she'd
never seen.

This second story is easier to tell because the whole family
has moved away, and because it has a happy, almost fairy-talish
end. It existed for me first *as* a story—my mother told it—and it
is important to me because it reminds me of girlhoods that happened all over the Bronx, fierce romances between mothers and
daughters in which a husband could only be a betrayal. I become
more comprehensible to myself when I hear these stories; they
belong to me, too.

The first story, though, which I've sketched despite a certain
heartsick guilt, matters to me more. The man himself is alone,
and writing about him feels like paying attention the way Willy
Loman's wife asks when she says, "Attention must be paid." Also,
our parents are still in touch; our own lives still feel close. I cannot fall under the illusion that because I remember this man from
long ago I understand him. At family gatherings he hovers at the
edge of awareness, the man who is absent. I want to write my way
into him. I want to fill him up with my words. I want to see him
by pouring my words into him, the way an iodine dye reveals a
system of veins.

The most difficult lives to write about—and the ones that
draw us most—are full of this same mystery and familiarity. They
are the ones where there is the greatest chance people involved
will read it and, despite disguises, recognize themselves. These
are the lives that brush against ours with a prickly closeness—
like someone standing right behind us, someone staring at us,
about to touch us, so that the hair on our neck rises instinctively.
We want to stop them. We want to see them.

Is it wrong to write about the living?

"If you want to be a writer, somewhere along the line you're
going to have to hurt somebody. And when that time comes, you

go ahead and do it," Charles McGrath said when he was an editor at *The New Yorker*. "If you can't or don't want to tell that truth, you may as well stop now and save yourself a lot of hardship and pain."

What sort of morality is this? That your own work is more important than someone else's suffering? That your own particular art is more important than your aunt or neighbor? And what if the writing is poor? What if the pain caused is just too intense for the person written about to bear?

A novelist wrote a withering account of her recent marriage. Soon after the book came out, the author's ex-husband killed himself. Was she correct to write that novel?

"The chief characteristic of an idol," Cynthia Ozick says, "is that it is a system sufficient to itself . . . It is indifferent to the world and to humanity . . . That dead matter will rule the quick is the single law of idolatry." If the story of your neighbor's life is more important than your neighbor herself, if the fossil of your neighbor's life, cast by the pressure of granite years, is more important than the actual person desperately trying to manage on the other side of the wall, then Art is a kind of god. It rises lustrous as some golden calf that shudders and sweats in firelight but by day remains aloof.

It is a sin to embarrass, the cantor of my girlhood synagogue taught. It makes blood surge to the victim's face, a rush of blood like a mini-death. God Himself proclaims, "None of you shall come near anyone of his own flesh to uncover nakedness." Leviticus lists all the various family relationships one must not violate by disclosure, and culminates with, "All who do any of these abhorrent things—such people shall be cut off from their people."

Cut off. This is alarming because along with forbidding incest, the rule against uncovering nakedness may mean do not write about what goes on behind closed doors, even if you've grown up behind them.

But my point is not that we should not write about the living. I bring up the Bible in order to acknowledge the deep-rooted nature of the taboo, why it can strike with such paralyzing strength.

Taboo, Freud points out, is a Polynesian word. Its meaning "branches off into two opposite directions. On the one hand it means to us, sacred, consecrated: but on the other hand it means, uncanny, dangerous, forbidden, and unclean."

Something harlequin, mixed, ambiguous, alloyed, hides in our twin desire and aversion to write about the living. It is not only the taboo person that we want to protect. We stretch out our hand to point, yet instantly snatch it back as if we saw it withered—like the wicked witch's feet gnarled up and then withdrawn when the beautiful ruby slippers are removed, like a skeletal finger in a horror movie: the flesh burnt off and the deeper human truth revealed.

The taboo has primal origins. It is, to some extent, implicit in being civilized. As we learn to talk we learn not to say what we see if it might cause hurt. Do not stare, darling. Do not point. He doesn't walk funny. You mustn't say that. We'll discuss it when we get home.

But at home, too, certain silences prevail. That slammed door? We have learned not to ask. That dark look? That whiff, perhaps, of alcoholic breath? We have learned to say nothing, even to ourselves. It is as if the unsaid had not occurred, and the less it is referred to, the more invisible it becomes until at last it vanishes into the texture of ordinary interaction like the mesh everything is woven on: all you see are the tidy stitches, the lovely picture they form.

The force of the forbidden draws us. We want its power. We want to use it for our work. We also long to understand the unarticulated, our own most potent reality not yet structured by words. For in fact the secrets we most want to understand are not secrets at all; they are nothing hidden so much as not yet discovered. They are what has been there all along, not furtively denied so much as never consciously noticed.

Taboo has two hands; it points opposite ways. It is like—to use another Oz image—the scarecrow at the crossroads, who by knotting himself calls attention to himself. He wishes to be freed. He wishes to be made whole, or rather *real*—that utmost desire of childhood. Children identify with their own toys; we all felt what it is to be a prop, an adjunct, a creature with eyes converted to flat buttons, and a mouth that is pretty, but sewn.

And now the page beckons.

Thin as the layer of silver that makes a mirror reflect, it urges, Set down here what you saw, and you will understand it as never before.

And so will all the world.

Lucille, a friend of mine, told me the story of the novelist's ex-husband. She told the story irritably, swinging her crossed leg. It suggested something, I think, that she wanted to believe and yet could not. And so she found it necessary to proceed without belief.

She had returned to writing after a long, uneasy time away, a time spent traveling, and editing a business journal she did not much care about, and gazing out the window at the other mothers her age advancing down the street behind silvery high-tech strollers.

Now that she was writing again, she took her work more seriously, and the more seriously she took it, the more she wrote about her family. She was in her late twenties and then her early thirties. She had a husband and a child, and she bore down on her writing as if it were a shovel stuck in the frozen ground that she must press on with all her might. She hung the weight of her whole life upon her words, honing them, honing them, until she broke the surface and brought up diamonds.

She was writing about being Asian-American, the daughter of immigrant parents. In one story a mother who remains in slippers and a robe all day insists her daughter practice the violin many hours each evening, although the girl now despises the instrument. Both mother and daughter seem to fear that without the violin, the girl will be nothing. Another story begins with a father removing his dentures. Quite precisely we are told the exact pulpy look of the father's mouth when he takes out the false teeth. The description is not gratuitous. It is essential to the story, which happens to end up underscoring the wisdom of the father which the adolescent daughter scorned. Still, when the story appeared in print, Lucille's father came to her.

He let her know that her writing about him pained him sometimes. He did not understand what he had done to her that she was so angry. He spoke for her mother, saying she also was disturbed. Please do not write about us anymore, he asked.

If my own father said this to me, I would feel in an absolute cauldron of guilt. My fantasies have always been to take lavish care of my parents as they grow older, and to make them proud of me. But could I give up writing about them if they asked?

Lucille refused. She loved her parents, but would not silence herself for them. If she could not write about what was most central to her, she told me later, she could not write at all. And yet, when she did write about them now, she said, she felt "like a ghoul."

My friend Regi set to writing essays. "Have you noticed," she inquired, "how if you let yourself write only nice things about people it ends up sounding like the kind of speech people give at a graveside? A eulogy, I mean? And how your writing really springs to life when you write something that, if they read it, they would *just die?*"

Again there is the suspicion that, in some sense, what's dead feeds on what's living, as if you are in Dr. Frankenstein's remote fortress lab, where your own mother, for instance, is strapped to one table and your blank book to the other. Again there is a strange confusion between what deserves to breathe and what deserves to be buried: character "assassinations" that violate the souls of the living, truths so deeply interred in living people's bodies that these people come to resemble figures of wax, yellowish, nerveless, like someone modeled out of calluses, as if the artificial person—the one who maintains a heavy fraudulence, stifling beneath a fog of perfume the most necessary truths—has become in herself a squat golden god, a Madame Tussaud effigy, rouged and lipsticked and propped in a corner, and you can imagine sticking pins in without causing pain. Death drifts from such a person, from the dry whole-wheat toast and the grapefruit halves, the puzzled frown at what nice people don't say, at what she herself refuses, it seems, to understand, so that it is tempting to see this mountainous pale figure as unfeeling, inert, molten candlestuff, laminated shut.

It is as if, in fact, the painful truth were a pin which the other person—one's mother, for instance—has swallowed deep within her, beneath layers and layers of herself. This hidden shard of truth is rigid as a stalactite, and one must force her to surrender it, opening her jaws and prizing it loose, because you need it to cut your own self free. It is as if the truth she's swallowed belongs to you, and as long as she denies what you've both seen, you cannot belong entirely to yourself; you are incredible, unreal, a magic slate whose sheet is lifted up again and again. ("I never, for a minute, resented you when you were a child." "Your sister adored you, always." "You gave my whole life meaning." "I did not send you away because I wanted to be rid of you. I only wanted you to be happy." Some examples of rubbery denial.) In later years, even if you bear down on your magic slate with emphatic force, pressing into the thick dark wax under the film—like writing into a plum or your own hand, trying to force the body to register its own experience—it doesn't matter. Out of habit, the gray film lifts. One detaches from what one felt, mistrusting it. Blankness returns.

We need confirmation from outside. We need to be seen and read aloud as if we were books in another's hands: our own ghostly thoughts set striding. How else can we become real? We reach toward the bones in our mother's ears, the malleus, incus, and stapes, small as thorns. We reach toward the spine, wanting its solidity. Our sword in the stone grows straight down through our parents. They are right to regard us with alarm.

My mother clipped my fingernails and burnt them over the gas stove when I was a child. I still recall the acrid smell, and the curling, blackening. She didn't want anyone to find my nails and make voodoo out of them. My friend Sandra in high school kept a clear medicine bottle of her nail clippings by her bed. There it was, a little walled place crawling with waxy slivers, the whitish nails scaling the vial, curling and tumbling among themselves, a bevy of moons, a packed cramped cell teeming with Sandra's body—she didn't want to throw them out perhaps for the same reason my mother didn't throw mine out, a terror of enemies, a lust to keep herself for herself and not to release even her debris into the world.

Freud describes a "taboo patient" who "adopted the avoidance of writing down her name for fear it might get into somebody's hands who thus would come into possession of a piece of her personality. In her frenzied faithfulness, which she needed to protect herself against the temptations of her phantasy, she had created for herself the commandment, 'not to give away anything of her personality.' To this belonged first of all her name, then by further application her handwriting, so that she finally gave up writing."

We must keep hold of our bodies because of what they might do if let loose. We must hoard our scraps of paper, and our scraps of nail, and transform our biting teeth into something a fairy can claim by setting them under our sleeping heads—letting our mothers have our teeth for the price of a candy, redeeming our bones for a dime, lying at our utmost vulnerable with the loose incisor beneath us so that, once we are dead to life, a switch can occur, and money and sweetness can console for the loss of our aggressive edge. It is an ancient belief: the body, sparked with passions, prison of all errant thoughts, is dangerous when free. It is, symbolically, the unconscious unchained. Split from rational control, it will do what it wants, betraying us.

Even what's dead of ours has a kind of life. And in our lives we experience patches of death, whole nights and days when we feel stuffed with sawdust, made of soaked skin like bandages, puffy, mummyish, fluttering off the frame. We die instead of feel. We worry our truths will kill. If we are mute, and bottle them up, perhaps they will kill only us.

So, who is the unfeeling wax figure? Who is the figure of Yellow Death? Is it the person who maintains a heavy fraudulence, or is it really one's own self? The emotionally deadened person seems calloused, insensate, reminiscent of drained wax bottles, the wax candy-soda bottles of childhood. We used to drink the sweet liquid—blue, red, green—then chew the loaf of wax: it was curious, like chewing one's own anesthetized mouth after the dentist, one's own mouth bereft of sensation, a big bloated fascinating thing like a sort of rubber goiter blooming off one's face, one's face pulled into an elastic, Silly Putty mockery of itself, a gargoyle of itself, the way my sister used to pull my face between viselike fingers, giving me a *kanip*, a savage double-pinch, while cooing, "Am I giving you conniptions?"—showing love while inflicting pain. Confusion smothered my feelings about her, and her true emotion remained invisible to me.

Which one of us was the figure who does not feel? Whose is the inert body one would force into consciousness? In writing about the living, aren't we trying to access something living in us, living incognito, interred, resisted, half-formed, sharp as a fang?

"I do not know what I have done to you that you are so angry at me," Lucille's father said.

His comment struck her as naive. This was just something she'd written. She was just using her material. And yet she would not surrender this material even for love. Without it—like the daughter with the violin—she feared she would be nothing.

Frankenstein, Mary Shelley's myth about bringing the dead to life, is in fact a parable about sacrificing family for the sake of artistic ambition. It reads like a transcript of our fears.

Young Victor Frankenstein goes far away. There's something he wants to know: the secret "of life." What exactly is the spark that makes creatures live? Excited by the rather prurient idea that scientists "penetrated into the recesses of nature and show how she works in her hiding-places," he stalks the graveyard; he dwells in the charnel-house. Taboo means nothing to him.

"My attention was fixed upon every object the most insupportable to the delicacy of human feeling," he says. "I saw how the fine form of man was degraded and wasted; I beheld the corruption of death succeed to the blooming cheek of life."

Only by examining what others shrink from—by viewing people's degradation and corruption, that is—can he hope to make his great discovery.

And yet his avowed aim is not to disparage, but rather to "pour a torrent of light on our dark world," much as James Joyce's artist hero, Dedalus, might have put it—as if art were a drenching sun; as if he hoped to open a deluge of illumination.

To do his work, Frankenstein must ignore his family. When he is in touch with them, when he so much as writes them a letter, he cannot go on. Being in touch with them puts him in touch with his own natural sense of horror, and he realizes what in fact his hands have been touching: things meant by all spiritual authority to be let rest underground.

So Frankenstein turns a deaf ear to his family, their anxious questions and pleas. "I knew well therefore what would be my father's feeling," he says, "but I could not tear my thoughts from my employment, loathsome in itself, but which had taken an irresistible hold of my imagination. I wished, as it were, to procrastinate all that related to my feelings of affection until the great object, which swallowed up every habit of my nature, should be completed."

How closely this mirrors the confession a writer once made to me! She had just published a novel based on her life and the lives of people she was close to, when she wrote this: "I realized very early on that if I was going to be worrying about what my parents or husband's ex-wife or stepchildren were going to think, if I wasn't going to be free to write the best book I could, whatever that meant in terms of possible hurt to people I was involved with, then I simply could not write that novel. So I shelved all the worries, figuring I'd deal with them later."

In Shelley's tale, which ends in such famous catastrophe, the artist's decision to ignore his family is not merely part of the problem; it is the problem. The author has Dr. Frankenstein proclaim, "If this law was always observed; if no man allowed any pursuit whatsoever to interfere with the tranquillity of his domestic affections, Greece had not been enslaved, Caesar would have spared his country . . . and the empires of Mexico and Peru had not been destroyed."

For as soon as Frankenstein has the knowledge he wants, he yearns to "author" (Shelley's word) fresh life. He cuts apart dead people, steals pieces, stitches these together, and then bestows the spark that makes his creature live. In other words, Frankenstein performs a physical analogue, a sort of physical enactment of imaginative writing. His project involves anatomical secrets; writers' work involves historical and psychological secrets. His work requires exhuming bodies; writers' work requires unburying events and emotions which have been suppressed. In both cases real people become mere material for the creator's ends.

And what happens when the work is done?

The instant Frankenstein's creature opens its eyes, its "author" is aghast. "The beauty of the dream vanished, and breathless horror and disgust filled my heart." Appalled, the doctor flees.

Why? Why isn't he delighted by his success? Why doesn't he think, okay, the creature's not so great to look at. In fact, it's ugly. But what's some yellow skin and black lips compared to what I've just accomplished? I made this thing live!

It's as if at last all the horror he's been suppressing is released. Or rather, it's as if all the emotions he repressed while working were actually going into his creation, which he now despises. The monster is the unconscious incarnate. It is the unconscious with hands and feet.

It stalks his "author" to his hometown. Here are the people Frankenstein always describes in idealized ways. For instance, there is Elizabeth, who his parents adopted when he was five, ending his status as his parents' only child and "idol." Elizabeth became his mother's favorite, and on her deathbed his mother extracted a promise that Frankenstein would marry her. Yet Frankenstein reports, "Everyone loved Elizabeth . . . Harmony was the soul of our companionship, and the diversity and contrast that subsisted in our characters drew us nearer together." Similarly rhapsodic about his general upbringing, he says, "No human being could have passed a happier childhood than myself. My parents were possessed by the very spirit of kindness and indulgence," etc.

At once, the monster slays Frankenstein's angelic youngest brother, and goes on to strangle Frankenstein's highly virtuous best friend. On Frankenstein's wedding night, the "demoniacal corpse" seizes Elizabeth, the bride, and chokes her to death. Frankenstein's aged father perishes of grief.

Once finished, the creation is beyond the author's control. It destroys all that he holds dear. When at last the creator himself dies, it is with relief. His agonizing guilt will finally end.

Shelley's story contains, in nightmare form, a writer's phantom fears. The melodrama of it—the thunder crashes, the feverish moonlit rooms—merely reflects the tenor of our repressed anxieties.

Frankenstein reports that he "disturbed, with profane fingers, the tremendous secrets of the human frame"—as if the hand obeyed its own rapacious morality. In fact, the monster's "signature" is strangling—he stifles all his victims, leaving "no sign of any violence except the black mark of fingers on [the] neck."

The beast seems to be body gone wild, the sin of immoral fingers conveyed through the flesh, as if how a thing is made is what it does, and an author's hand will communicate to his or her work all sorts of secret messages, whorling, cross-hatched, gouged inscriptions, willow trees and angel's heads, that it will in turn reveal as it travels through time. There are secrets within secrets that even the writer merely suspects.

I am looking not for objective truth but for emotional truth. I am looking for the way writing about the living feels when we feel its dangers most forcefully, when we wake at 4 A.M. dreading what we have done during the day and what its repercussions will be.

What we feel at 4 A.M. we also feel at 10 A.M. but with this difference: the day casts a sort of scrim before it so that the hunched form that pursues us is diffused, wrapped in haze. At 4 A.M. the light shines straight through, showing the stalker in all its clarity. Better turn and see who it is. Maybe there is something the gnarled, tenacious form is trying to say.

When I was growing up my family had a secret. My sister was fat. It was the one thing you were not allowed to say. In an argument you might say many nasty things, but never this. It would be too painful. It would kill her. She could never forgive you. It was too mean. And yet it was the most obvious thing about her, maybe the most important. It seemed implicated everywhere in her life: who her friends were, whether she came straight home from school or went to the Fordham Road library by herself, and whether she rode the 100 bus or trudged up the long Kingsbridge hill to our house on foot to save the twenty cents for an ice cream, and what that ice cream meant, and how much she spoke at the dinner table, and if you were allowed to interrupt.

It was implicated too somehow in those energetic Saturday afternoons spent whipping up big batches of bread and kolaches from scratch, and in my mother's complaints about the value of the half-dozen fresh white eggs she mixed in, the cupfuls of sifted flour, the butter—melted, "clarified," to a flowing gold, and then worked into the heavy mass of batter in the bowl— what it meant when, vexed by my mother's remarks, and in a tearful fury, she grabbed the bowl and marched down the building corridor and heaved it all—purchased ingredients and afternoon's intent and pleasured labor—down the incinerator. Gone. My mother gazed at me and bit her lip. My sister walked past us and flung shut the bathroom door. We heard her turn the lock, and then, sobbing, wrench apart thick magazines—my mother's *Vogue*, the library's *Cosmopolitan*—and with each sizzling rip it was as if she were tearing flesh. All this had to do somehow with Anita's weight.

Of course in a way there was no need to discuss it. It was what one could not for a moment forget. By not discussing it, though, it was as if one must see Anita but not see her. We saw her and didn't see her, we spoke to her and didn't speak to her, we loved her for who she was and we refused to acknowledge who she was. Are all secrets this obvious? I recall her at a street corner—she had just stepped off the number 10 bus and was walking slowly in her oatmeal cloth coat and molded shoes up the street. She walked like an old woman. Her body was like a heavy, doleful burden she must advance. How bright the pavement was! How slow and steady were her feet!

At writing school I wrote a story about two sisters. One of them was fat. This was the first thing I wrote when I got to writing school, far away from Riverdale, in the scorched Midwest. Everyone was worried that the corn in the fields was burning from the sun's force. Afternoons, it was so hot you could almost smell char in the rare breeze. The skies were as open as plate glass, the color of wheat. I walked around euphoric and dazed. I saw a pig. I thought it was the most exotic thing I'd ever seen. I bought a wooden bowl and a cookbook, but ate frozen fishsticks almost every night. Because I'd never eaten them before, these too seemed exotic. Those first nights, in a small, tight efficiency apartment that looked like a motel and smelled of the vinyl pull-out couch and the new brown and blue rug, my knees locked into the keyhole of the student desk, the air spinning with the grinding of cicadas, a sound I'd never heard before in my life, all I could think about was the Bronx, and being nine, and singing rounds with my sister when we brought her home from Andre Clark Girl Scout Camp.

"My ears are plugged up with my fingers," was the first sentence I wrote there. My second and third were: "My voice sounds muffled and echoey, like singing into a bottle, and the entire time there's a seashell hum in the background and at the end of it, Anna's tiny voice singing my tune before I reach it. It's a round, and if I don't keep my ears shut I get confused and end up singing Anna's part."

Now it strikes me that this first writing had to do with voice, with trying to be deaf to oneself so as not to sound like someone else. At the time, though, I knew just that I wanted to write about Anita. At last, far away, in what seemed like the most alien place although it was the heartland, I turned to her. I assumed she would never read a word I wrote. It was like writing with milk, with invisible ink, in a diary locked with a key I'd swallow.

"Hmm. It doesn't come to much," my writing teacher said, but I knew it had come farther than I'd thought possible. It started in Briarcliff Manor, New York, and ended on my own doorstep on Johnson Avenue, and in that it had come farther than my writing had ever come before.

Obscurity would swallow these stories, I thought, and so protecting Anita from them did not concern me. If I published them, they would be in journals no one had heard of, under a name that did not yet exist. Actually, though, I thought little of publication. I was always on to something else. I wrote quickly, that first semester, in a room that was innocuous, anonymous. At night I fantasized I was in Alaska, in Tuscaloosa, someplace far. The room was a box with a window under a black sky. You couldn't hear so much as a car whoosh past. I wrote into obscurity; it accepted all I gave. I could write anything, yet what I did write was more and more about the character Anna. And gradually I realized I wanted to write a novel.

The novel I had planned was about disease in a family. My own sister not only was fat, but had developed multiple sclerosis. It was just a tingling in her elbow at first, a pins-and-needles that would not go away, as if just that part of her had fallen asleep and was perpetually in the process of waking up. Pins-and-needles, and then a clumsiness of the hand, and then a drag of the foot. At her wedding she moved stiff as a robot down the aisle in thick white shoes like nurse's shoes, leaning on our parents. Her dress, which my mother chose off the rack at Macy's, was knee-length, so it wouldn't interfere. Anita had asked for no dancing at her wedding because she could not dance. Instead, a man played electronic keyboard, Muzak versions of "We've Only Just Begun" and "Sunrise, Sunset" that were surprisingly pleasant. At one point I noticed Anita sitting by herself. Everyone else was up and mingling, but she could not get to her feet without help. She sat alone, in the middle of the long linen-covered laminated-wood table, her elbow raised awkwardly as she spooned cantaloupe into her mouth while she gazed down at her plate. In a moment I was up and rushing to her, but still that earlier glimpse of her remained.

I wanted my novel also to include scenes that showed in precise detail what this disease did to her body and mind. How could I write about what I saw? It was a shame, the sort you drop your eyes from. You do not stop and point. I wanted to stop and point. I wanted to point so the whole world would see. I did not want the world to drop their eyes from her. I wanted to transcribe the exact creak of her aluminum walker as she approaches my parents' apartment for Friday night supper on the days she's well enough to walk, the exact same corridor she bolted down as a girl, rushing from the incinerator. I wanted to transcribe the exact thump of the rubber-tipped legs of the walker she casts before her, and the precise metallic rasp as she leans on it, and the rough swish of her slippers as she drags her stony feet. One of her feet, twisted perpetually out, must be lifted over the threshold for her. My mother cuts her chicken for her; she can no longer wield a knife. Since Anita spends almost all day alone in her apartment, sitting in the worn gold-velour chair my father gave her, she doesn't have many things to talk about. She tells about reruns of "Mystery!" and "Hawaii Five-O," and her conversation with the man at Short Story International when she called to renew her subscription, and about the fact that when she was at City College she took calculus for fun—"for fun, mind you!" she repeats, brandishing the handle of her fork, because, she says, she had a highly organized mind and liked to use it. She eats little. She used to be a great reader—reading was her escape—but now manages only two or three pages a day. Her disease blurs vision in a way glasses can't fix. One day she said to me, "I'm having so much trouble seeing. I need a stronger prescription. Do you think it's possible for grease from your hair to get on your eyes?" When she sits, arms drooped in her lap, she looks hunched. Her body is prone to "accidents"—the reek of urine, her anxious glance: oh, the humiliation! I wanted to write it all down.

Why? I wanted to say, simply, this happpened. It seemed almost horrible that others did not know, that the world had not responded to it. How did I expect the world to respond? I didn't know. Only, the rest of the world seemed heartless for not knowing the truth of Anita's life. In part, fury made me want to press Anita's story in people's faces. It actually seemed to me that the world could not hear the truth of Anita's life and continue as it had. Something would have to change. And I wanted to challenge God. I had selected an epigram for my unwritten novel. "Should not the Judge of the world deal justly?"—Genesis 18:25.

I thought I wasn't religious, but when I wrote about multiple sclerosis, God appeared. There He was, indicted. The world's beauty had never sent me looking for explanations; it was the botches that suggested God's signature, as if He'd gotten careless blotting His pen, as if, in neglect or rage for some inscrutable reason, He'd left the ink nub to pool darkly on the page. Sometimes my own sister seemed like Frankenstein's monster, and Frankenstein was God, or, if I wrote about her, Frankenstein was me.

In the novel I planned, I wanted to examine not only an older sister's disease, but a younger sister's response. I imagined a plot in which the older sister comes to live with the younger when her body worsens, much as I feared my own sister would come to live with me. To the younger sister I gave many riches: a country house made of a renovated barn, a teaching job at the state university, a baby, and a husband who would be understanding up to a certain point.

The older sister, in my plot, would come to dominate the life of the younger. There would be a bitter scene at supper when the older accused the younger of coldness and selfishness, and a scene in which the younger realized her sister, occupying the bedroom next door, could probably hear her having sex, and there would be a third during which the older sister was jealous of the infant, and complained bitterly about her. Tensions would develop in the younger sister's marriage. A choice would have to be made. Will the younger sacrifice herself for the older, to save the older going into a nursing home? Added to this would be scenes of closeness between the two sisters, occasions of intimacy greater than any friend or even husband could achieve.

It was a dark book I had planned. It made out of my history my future—issues of domination and self-sacrifice had overrun my life with my sister, growing up. Her rages and griefs, the tyrannical hold she could exert over an entire household—all this the page would register, as well as our passionate love for each other. And yet this story seemed too mean to write. Even simply describing the disease seemed heartless.

"M.S. stands for three things," my sister once said at Friday supper. All soup spoons paused in mid-air—she always had a knack for commanding attention. "Ms., manuscript, and multiple sclerosis." She looked at me.

Ah, of course. And in my mind those three are linked: being an autonomous woman with a right to value and transcribe her own experience, writing the body of the manuscript itself, and having the disease my sister is afflicted with, a multiple sclerotic hardening that leaves dull scar tissue where there was once a filigree of fine nerves.

Gradually, the ms. I wrote in a way replaced her M.S. I thought, at the time, I shouldn't talk to her too much. I might be tempted to write down just what she'd said that morning rather than maintaining the psychic distance to write the best scenes I could. When I'm done writing this, I thought, I'll spend more time with Anita. I was dealing with her life by putting it in a book. I kept my pages in a room I went into only when I wrote. I kept the door shut. My monster lived in there.

"I believe my writing is good enough to be punished, I mean *published*," I once said.

In fact, I never wrote the book I planned. I got as far as the foreword, and then turned back to the characters' childhoods, where I remained. I came to love this other book, this unplanned book, and a friend, hearing parts of it, said to my surprise that all the same issues were in there anyway, call them obesity, call them M.S., call them jealousy and stigma and love and guilt.

I didn't trust I could do my sister justice. Writing nonfiction about her disease feels different. As long as I make up nothing, as long as I record as accurately as I can exactly what I witness, then I feel I am respecting Anita. However, I am not comfortable letting my imagination subsume it or distort it, even in the interests of making a more effective scene.

Why? That feels like colluding with God, or with whatever circumstance determined that she would have this disease, in giving it to her. It feels like I am inventing troubles for her. And there's something too sacred, too powerful about the truth to do what feels like playing with the facts, even if it is not really play. I do not want to risk distortion or burlesque. God commanded that Lot and his wife not look back at the cities of Sodom and Gomorrah, which He saw fit to incinerate. Lot strode forward, toward his long life, despite the smell of ash and the shrieks that must have filled the air. But his wife, nameless, rebelled. She looked back at God's destruction, at a face of His she was not supposed to see, and was instantly transformed to salt, her whole being a tear with the liquid burnt off. Some things we cannot see and afterward live unharmed. But if we see these things I think we ought to leave an accurate monument, even if it is just a monument of salt.

I wish I could have written the novel I wanted to. I wish I'd had more respect for my own feelings and vision. I wish I were my younger self come to visit my older. I'd say, "Dive in. Write those hardest scenes first. Of course they'll feel like they're veering out of control. Of course you'll wonder if you'll ever get it right. Do it, and do it over." It is not a sin to write one's truth. We have an obligation to the living, but this includes the person living within us, whom we may never know if we do not let her speak.

The friend who shelved her worries so she could write her autobiographical novel told me, "I think it's essential to set yourself outside that sphere of personal consequence for the space of the writing, to free yourself, to forgive yourself, and write what's most true—what's so often both the ugliest and the most beautiful."

Dedalus teaches how to track to the very core of the labyrinth where the half-human beast lives, the rejected, voracious, monstrous child of royal birth, and then how to return to the outside world again without getting lost (all one needs is a length of thread, a spool of words). Inward, inward one travels. Roars echo out. Dead ends and blind passageways, and wild glimpses in sudden mirrors. Dare you go? Have you a right? Dedalus stands for the kind of person who is "dedicated to the morals not of his time but of his art," Joseph Campbell writes. He adds, "He is the hero of the way of thought—singlehearted, courageous, and full of faith that the truth, as he finds it, shall make us free."

At the beginning of its life, Frankenstein's monster was actually a gentle, loving creature. It was the doctor's constant rejection that drove it savage with loneliness. Our monsters may turn to blessings if we regard them with kindness. They may have been blessings from the start, made goblins in the shadowy hallways of our minds. "To deny one's own experiences is to put a lie into the lips of one's own life. It is no less than a denial of the Soul," Oscar Wilde writes. How fine it would be to fully claim our eyes and ears and mouths, to say, "This is what I see. This is what I hear. And this is how I say it. Listen: I say it like this."

THE PARAFFIN DENSITY
OF WAX WINGS:
WRITING SCHOOL

W HEN I WENT TO WRITING SCHOOL, I craved rules. I craved a mentor, and the revelation of secrets, and the permission to write scads, and most of all I craved the confirmation that I could write. In other words, I was like practically everyone else.

What a mystique writing programs have! A sense of promise emanates from their doors, wafts up from the embossed paper bearing their letterheads. I felt that being accepted to one, and especially to that bizarrely exotic one nestled in the middle of America, Iowa, was like being chosen for an initiation into mysteries. After all, what could be more mysterious than learning how to write? A friend of mine had gone there. I received a postcard back from her crammed with tiny type. It pictured a man in a straw hat driving a mule-led wagon, and on the back the remark that her writing had undergone a quantum leap in excellence. And this was just October.

In February I visited her and gazed at the bowl of warty gourds on her vast farmhouse table and the typewriter covered with a deep blue silk scarf, like a tarot deck. At 5 A.M. I walked the boarded sidewalks of Oxford (population 660), the town outside Iowa City where my friend lived, inhaling the odor of manure as if it were perfume, too thrilled to sleep, standing beneath a sky that was absolutely the biggest thing I had ever seen, and perhaps the clearest, while a truck that was also of colossal proportions bore down on me, I noticed, at an astonishing pace. It emitted a roguish honk that banged back from the heavens and shimmered away over the fields, and that left me, after the thing itself vanished in a tide of dust, feeling inordinately calm, as if nothing would ever be able to surprise me again. Behind me the town of Oxford looked like the set of a Western: five or six storefronts facing a single street. I walked onto the set and slipped into the door that was ajar.

My friend was frying eggs. A scratchy old Dylan tape played on her cassette player, hard-bitten lyrics with a fiddle reeling wildly in the background. I sat at the table and gazed at my friend's bookcase. It was filled with slender volumes of contemporary poetry. She hardly used to own any poetry, being a believer in libraries. Now she possessed all this. While I helped cook, my eyes kept returning to those slim books, and, because I could hardly understand even their names, they appeared to me as rare and foreign as slivers of gold shaved from distant domes.

Men came over, and a woman or two. We had brunch. We drank. My friend was dating a soft-spoken ginger-haired second-year who was a "TWIF," a Teaching-Writing Fellow, the rank given those few whom Iowa deemed its absolute best. This man had a roommate, Jackson, a poet who had already published. He was the first Southerner I'd ever met. He said "po-eem," and "woe-m'n," and we argued about possessiveness, I maintaining the absurd position that a poet should be able to steal any line from another poet if it resulted in better art. I wondered what his parents said about his work. He said he had stopped showing them his writing years ago. He asked about my bus trip from Chicago. I told about the green windows, the highway set between vast fields, the gargantuan McDonald's, the woman in a pink felt hat who told the driver that she was going to visit her two sisters in Dubuque, and how the driver waited in his seat while the three old women linked arms, stepped off the curb, and crossed the road before him. "Three sisters," he announced. Jackson gazed at me, and I thought, This is what it feels like to be a storyteller. This is it, at last.

I attended a poetry workshop and then a fiction workshop. The poetry workshop was actually at the poet's house. At one point the poet stuck out his arms and said, "Okay. I'm the tree. The birds are here, and here," gesturing to one arm and then to the top of his head as he tried to show us how one of the poems on the worksheet quite literally did not make sense. To my friend, who had written an exquisite poem set in medieval China and reminiscent of Ezra Pound, he said little. He merely wondered why she chose to write poems set in medieval China these days. I was surprised. What did he want? My friend shrugged, but seemed to understand.

The fiction workshop was less focused. People discussed a few of the sentences here and there in the story. No one seemed that interested. The people who did speak spoke in a very slow dry way, their throats raspy, their remarks trailing off as if they had become too depressed to finish. When the break came I walked out a door at the end of the hallway. It gave onto a gravel roof. The sky was brittle blue. Inhaling was like drinking cold water fast. I wished it would numb the aroused way I'd felt ever since I arrived in Iowa. I gulped and gulped, and then skipped the second half of the workshop to get a walk-in haircut.

The haircut cost six dollars. I watched the beautician's hands fly swiftly all over my head and hoped I would end up looking marvelous, but no. I looked like myself with less hair. Ever since I had come to Iowa I was writing on every scrap of paper I could find. I had drunk so much wine I awoke still drunk, although perhaps it was just excitement that made me feel that way. Am I drunk, I wondered, or is it Iowa? It's Iowa, it's Iowa, I thought. And applied to the school right away.

I arrived with a vast manuscript I had worked on for two and a half years. Parts of it were written longhand, parts of it were typed, parts of it still existed only in my head. It had no name. It had no end. I had been writing it the entire time I lived in Boston, in a room off an endless corridor. Doors swung open and closed. The smell of nail polish, burnt coffee, Ban deodorant spray, Chanel drifted in. Everyone had her own schedule. Not even the phone ringing bothered me. When I had first come to Boston I bought a massive gray industrial metal desk and wedged it by the window. This desk looked indestructible. You could stab this desk with scissors and knives, or kick it with a steel-toed boot, and it would make no difference. I sat down and wrote on my novel at this desk every morning. Sometimes I glanced up and the sapling outside was in leaf. Sometimes I glanced up and it was bare. The alarm clock burst into a frantic buzzing at noon, and I set down my pen and stepped into my skirt and heels and departed for the Mutual of New York Life Insurance Company. The building had sealed windows that tinted the world outside a brownish gold, and hidden vents that hummed with the perpetual exhalation of processed air. As I stood filing insurance policies into a green metal cabinet, rubbing one itchy stockinged leg with the toe of my shoe, I wondered what my life meant. Then I thought of that day's pages, the bit of episode I'd dreamed forward.

At Iowa I crammed as much of the manuscript as I could into a spring-back binder, and gave it to my teacher. I thought, Whatever she says about that book I will absolutely believe. I wanted to be absolved of having to believe in my own book by myself any longer. I felt light and hopeful while I waited for her response. Everything I did—chopping broccoli, reading Willa Cather, listening to a story about Bible camp written by a new friend—partook of this same feeling of detached suspense, as if my job right now was to keep my attitude benign.

"Come in," came my teacher's basso voice when I knocked on her door after two weeks. Hers was a blank door, with just her name printed on an index card in a firm, neat hand. She sat facing the cinderblock wall. There was my manuscript, on the desk. She slid it back to me, and told me three things.

"Please turn to page 127," she said.

The word "I" had been circled every time it appeared on the page.

"How many circles are there?" she asked.

I counted fourteen. The page nearly jumped and jostled with circled I's. But I was not sure what to make of this. Every time I'd written "I," I meant "I." Was it wrong to mean "I" so much? Or did the problem have to do with the word itself? Ought I find a synonym—*is* there a synonym?—for "I"? But no, I suspected the problem ran deeper.

The second thing she said to me was to please look at the comments on the back of page 32. These were comments my earlier teacher had written. He was a conscientious instructor for an extension school class that met in a suburban library. "Those are good comments," she said. "I suggest you do exactly what they say." I was surprised. If that teacher was as good as Iowa, why had I come?

The third and last thing she told me was, "Every writer has a book they do not publish. This," she said, "will be yours." She glanced at her watch, and stood.

"Thank you very much. Thank you," I said, stumbling for the door. Five minutes had elapsed.

Once upon a time I was sure I knew exactly what this story meant. She was a bad teacher. She was mean. Even if the manuscript were terrible, certainly there was more she could teach about a piece that was hundreds and hundreds of pages long. Why, two years later another writer on the faculty spoke about the book encouragingly for over an hour, although while she was speaking I realized that the novel was for me by then effectually dead.

Perhaps this first teacher, dismayed, thought, Why try to convey the whole workshop in one meeting? Then too, there was the business of her irritation, for I felt her irritation as soon as I walked in. At the time I took it for granted, but now I wonder,

Whatever was it doing with us in that room? Was it the irritation of feeling your ears have been chewed off, of encountering a narrator who just won't go away, of having to sit across from a student with shining eyes and a terribly hopeful manner and a big book that at the moment seems to personify a bloated ego or some voracious personal demand, and having to say the very things she will most hate to hear? And what had all that to do with me?

I wept, and resolved immediately to begin writing short stories. Everyone here wrote short stories. Maybe stories would teach me what I needed to learn. I threw my novel into a corner, where it lay for a long time like a shameful body part that another person could not bear to regard for more than five minutes.

I had learned my first grand lesson of writing school. It had to do with power, and belief.

What we learn most deeply is usually what we do not know we are learning at all. Years later, if we are lucky, we recognize the shape of what we have learned, its true anatomy. Writing school was like that. I always thought I was learning something multiple and complicated, when I was learning something singular and simple. I attended so avidly to particular lessons—when to use the simple past tense, when to suppress the narrator's emotion—that I did not notice the grand lessons that I took in unconsciously.

I wrote stories. Almost everyone I knew wrote stories. The one woman I knew who was writing a novel soon shaped each chapter into a short story. She came over, clattering through the streets of Iowa City in high heels and a pillbox hat, and toting Parliament's and a red plastic pocketbook and flurries of pages scrawled in her wire-bound notebook. She read aloud in a voice withered by smoke and sleeplessness and by pure will. (I once asked her if she would care to swim with me. "Swim?" she asked, looking at me askance. "Honey, these lungs are shot." She was twenty-five.) Nevertheless, she was the best reader I had ever heard. She gave each word perfect, weighted dignity, so that you yearned to hear her read a soup can, to know if even that most banal list could withstand the measured drama of her voice. She was a cross between Joan Didion, Mae West, and Eloise of the Plaza Hotel—fragile and urbane, a child in a scoop-neck dress— and did not weather the Workshop well. Criticisms assailed her like a cloud of gnats. She scratched and clawed blindly, explaining and defending and firing excuses before the critique was half out of the other student's mouth (this was outside of workshop; in workshop she sat blinking, her crossed leg bobbing like wild), so that you sensed both how utterly she refused to let her work be imperfect, and how despairing she was of ever, ever getting her work right.

She had come to Iowa, she once confided, in possession of a letter from Scribner's. Did she have a novel? the letter asked. If so, please send it. She had published a short story in the magazine *Ploughshares*, a ribald, rowdy story featuring some college students who were friends. The Scribner's letter stemmed from that, but its glow diminished as the semesters wore on, so that, by graduation, although she finished the novel and typed it up in thesis format (*Autumn Song*, I think the elegiac title ended up being), it was with a sense of something disappearing down a well. Her temperament was ill-suited to critiques. Something eroded in her as the months passed so that eventually her play-anemia approached the waxy fatigue of real anemia, and the dark glasses she now wore didn't seem a chic accessory. Her father had not wanted children, she told me on one of the rare afternoons we spent together that second year. He was jealous of the attention they took from his wife. "Is that so?" I said, sensing she'd given me one of the skeleton keys to her life. But it was late afternoon, and I was tired of drinking her coffee. I left before she told me much else.

*   *   *

Yet it was at Iowa that I became a writer. Before I went there, I wrote, but blindly. I had no idea what I put on the page. Words came in a flood. I gushed, and never looked back. I could write a chapter a day. I didn't see what was the big deal. Of course, sometimes I stopped to groom a sentence, brushing it up so it plumped and shone with many attractive words. But I rewrote nothing. Why should I? Hadn't I said what I meant?

This was the problem with the novel. It was like a file cabinet that is all one file. It got going and it just went, over hill and dale, around and around the block, like an electric toy with a tireless battery, never quickening or slowing or ever acknowledging it had seen these sights before. I wrote the same thing over and over because I didn't trust it had communicated. And I thought, The more words the better. People read because they enjoy reading. Wouldn't they enjoy reading more words more?

Writing school worked as a marvelous brake. It slowed me powerfully. It allowed me to see exactly what I was doing. People had, in fact, been advising more slowness for years. In a Spanish course at college, the teacher beckoned after class. "We are all intelligent here," he said. "When you speak, pay attention to your grammar." My face blazed. It was true: when I spoke I cared only about getting my idea across. I was still at the age when one thinks the idea itself—freshly invented—is what is extraordinary, and that it must be told fast before it vanishes. Spanish became just a bothersome obstacle, like a stile to a galloping horse.

Writing school turned out to be all about grammar, the grammar of fiction, the syntax and inflection of rhetorical choices. "Strategy" was talked about a lot here, as if a story consisted of troops on various maneuvers. How did you deploy your forces? How did you manage your subject's inherent strengths, and compensate for its weaknesses? No longer was your story something bodied forth in a sort of rapture; no longer was it something as natural and mysterious to you as your own foot. Now it was revealed to be a series of specific choices: why this phrase here, why that explanation there, was this ending "earned" or was it a bit of fancy eloquence glued on, like a false facade on a house? You couldn't answer. The story itself had to provide all its reasons. What it couldn't justify remained troublesome, dubious, a bit of "indulgence," even—so that you realized there was a morality to telling, and that everything in a story must be in the service of its final shape.

It started to become clear how strong writing got strong. Your eyes counted more than you'd known, and your hands and tongue and the shivery sensitivity of your skin. Your vocabulary counted less. All those years of collecting words, assuming by themselves they'd get you out of any jam! Words had been my abracadabra, and I'd hoarded them in little bound books, prying them from novels and reviews like arrowheads, amulets, charms whose use I would live to discover. Rows of words stacked one below the other and descending through the rococo flourishes of their third and fourth gradations of meaning—all because I knew that one day I would be baffled, stopped before a locked door, and at that moment the "shazam" might occur to me from out of the archives. Words were tricks, and I meant to know lots of them. At Iowa I saw that all those words led me no closer to real writing. They reeked of the library and secondhand life, and of the shiny red apple placed on the teacher's desk, and which holds on its laminated skin a tiny blue window in which one sees oneself looming, looming, unable to get out of one's own way.

Phi Beta Kappa counted for nothing here. Theoretical methodology counted for nothing, too. One of the finest writers was a shaggy man without college who said he slept in a tent pitched in his living room for fear that a turtle would crawl on his head. He spoke his stories into a tape and a secretary he paid typed them, ineptly. Broken glass, a yellow dress, a swing rushing up to the sky carrying a boy who at last leaps, a woman in a doorway bleeding from the mouth—who cared what this writer's philosophy was? Days later you noticed you still had his story in your head. He had what lots of us work to learn: a shucked vividness, as if he'd peeled the world's things and seen their pulp.

Sometimes I felt my earlier education had ruined me. I'd shunned the world to get at books. Now I saw books milked the world; they thrived on it. The world was pressed between their pages, like the leaves my sister saved in the encyclopedia. Two decades later I looked up "Abyssinia" and a leaf fluttered out: mustard-green, crushed thin as foil but brittle, its veins risen to the surface like an old person's. What mad thought possessed a girl to stuff a tree into the World Book, what longed-for hope? Was it for this? This startling autumn? This memento mori from Girl Scouts? At writing school I found books were lined with the world; it was pressed into them, crammed into them until the bindings bulged. Writing set me back in the world the way reading never had.

Although what mattered was not the world, but how you used it. How convincing was this dialogue? Why was this scene prolonged by three relatively plodding sentences? The elderly mother in the story—wasn't it going too far to give her liver spots, a trembling neck, *and* teary eyes? One should be cut: the neck or the eyes, preferably. "Sincerity is technique," a friend quoted Auden, and now I understood: technique was how to achieve sincerity. Did you care deeply, deeply about your subject? That was nothing. What mattered was how your story read.

"What rich material you have!" came to seem the most condescending remark possible. The world was strewn with material. Like dust, it was everywhere. If your material bunched uncomfortably, if you stitched and snipped it with ease, if it crimped like haute couture or draped like the most natural garment on earth—that was its worth. The same material could make melodrama, or strike with hushed truth. The same material could generate scenes so vaporous, so fogged with verbiage, that the reader emerged merely irritated, as if he'd been blindfolded for an hour while someone whispered excitedly in his ear. Or it could set you quite simply in the middle of events, so that when a woman entered you saw her, and when the narrator drank old coffee it was old coffee, sludgy and bitter, in your own mouth. What was

sex, even? Written one way, it made you wish to shut the door
and daydream; written another, you wanted never to see a naked
body again. Even God was only as strong as you wrote Him. Here
truly was the promised magic. It was taught here, after all—and it
was almost all that *was* taught here. Its name was technique.

One much-envied woman wrote sentences like mute faces.
They meant several things at once or else they meant nothing at
all. They had a killing grace. Reading them, you never thought
of a person writing them; they seemed to have dropped straight
from heaven or rolled off an assembly line. This writing was all
the rage. Emotion existed in these stories like a distant moon, a
pathology, a suicide the narrator had recovered from. They were
complicated pieces, with an iron beauty that locked itself into
your memory.

As did their author. She sat amid a torrent of red hair, circling around and around with her Bic pen in her notebook while
her work was discussed, and chewed Bazooka bubblegum. The
candy smell drifted through the room: cherry, grape. One day as I
stood in a long line outside the bursar's office I heard this woman
shout, "I don't have time for this!" It was an altercation with a
dean. She held a slip of green paper in her hand—it needed sig-
natures—and rattled it, incensed. Then she swept past. I
thought, Why is her time so important? What does she mean to
do with it? My own line inched forward. If my time were more
important to me, I wondered, would I write stories like hers? For
her soul was in them, apparently, even if it was hidden. She cared
passionately about the hours of her life, and so she must care
about her pages, even if the blaze in her stories was invisible.

Another man wrote stories that always led to white space.
There would be some paragraphs and then a poignant rim of
white space gaping like an antiseptic wound, as if speech could
only go so far before mute agony intervened. This man ended up
working for Hallmark. Occasionally, buying an anniversary card
or a birthday card, I wonder about him.

Here, in both writers, was a style dedicated to technique. It was technique as triage, as refuge, as glittering fortress, and yet in its commitment to form this way of writing taught tremendously.

Stories are machines inhabited by a god. School pointed out the cranks and spindles. It showed how to get the most leverage possible by grasping the jack-handle at the farthest point. It taught me to recognize grit in the system, the tiny distracting particles that can draw the whole thing to an abrupt halt—a wobbly point-of-view, a pompous phrase. The method was mostly cautionary; it was easier to see where a story was broken than where it ran smooth.

The god part, though, remained unmentioned. That was the writer's own business. How you wrote, where your ideas came from—everything that preceded class scrutiny of a piece went unacknowledged. This was writing school but we did not talk about writing. We talked about what had got written. We came to find it faintly embarrassing to hear how these words came to be on this page. The writer's vision, the vocabularies we wished to dwell in, the hints of dreams and memories that haunted the edge of our work—verboten, not discussed. We had come here because as children we'd clasped books to ourselves, running down the streets laughing after reading a particularly marvelous sentence in a particularly exciting scene, thinking, This is the best book in the world!—before, gasping, we stopped on a street corner to read on. We had come here because one day, bent over a sheet of yellow, green-lined paper, we smiled, having just then rendezvoused with ourselves like a Doppler effect of two waves surging into a big wave twice their height. How to have this pleasure more? How to turn on the switch in ourselves that made writing possible? How to transform the texture of life—the heat shimmer of a highway in which everything attenuates and billows skyward, every solid thing a form of smoke—into the lucid corridors and conclusions of a short story? How to write despite fear? Questions we did not ask.

On Thursday or Friday afternoon, and sometimes as late as Monday morning, a stack of copies of a stapled, Xeroxed story appeared on the workshop shelf. The Xerox machine was tired, and tended to erode the type, so that the stories we read were printed in wavery, broken letters in a field of dust, as if the words were receding from us. We read with pen in hand. We discussed the overall impact of the story, whether the story "worked"—the way a magic trick may or may not "work"—and all the various moves of the author along the way. Every choice was questioned. Our talk was technical, respectful. Like scientists, we did not ask how the creator functioned, but what he or she had done.

I, for one, managed to do only less and less. I wrote some sentences, studied them, and wrote them over again. Meaning drained from them while I worked. When all the meaning was gone I set my writing aside for the day and took a walk. My brain felt like a wad of chewed gum. I gaped at the simple reality of a tree. The point of all this work was not to banish meaning. Quite the contrary: it was to find the optimal arrangement of words to convey the most meaning possible. I wanted to arrive at words just saturated with meaning, but it was a crooked path that led there. The goal was a sort of perfection, and I could see that the only hope of arriving at this perfection was by way of revision. Revision, I realized, allowed an ordinary intelligence to achieve greatness. Through revision even a sloppy writer could achieve the tailored figure of elegance. And yet, since there was a sort of salvation to be found in revision, it was, ironically, easy to get lost in it, too.

It could, in fact, take on a compulsive energy of its own. The first time I took a bath as a young teenager (we had moved from an apartment where I took only showers), I stepped out of the tub and rubbed a towel against myself. Suddenly I saw little gray nubbly growths all over me—rolls of dirt! They were the size of pinky nails, rolled up like minuscule cigars. The more I rubbed to get rid of the dirt, the more dirt appeared. It seemed to generate from within me, like parthenogenesis. Frightened, I called my mother, who told me, "Honey, that's *skin*."

Rubbing away at a story, every word can look like dirt. You

brush eraser dust from the page and stare again at an incident that appears less and less familiar, wound through as it is with blank white, becoming, you hope, more and more perfect, more and more timeless, as if before your eyes condensing into an artifact—and yet somehow leaving you and all you meant behind. Is this what you came for? Is this why you write? As if beauty were death. As if art holds life in contempt. As if when you yourself have been utterly expunged, it will be complete.

A whole season might net just one story, a story carved through so many drafts it dwindled limply, scarcely alive, its heart grafted to its lungs, its arms and legs missing entirely. One regarded such botches amazed. Love had engendered it. Conception had come all in a wild heat. Yet here the thing lay after weeks of surgical concern, barely recognizable. One suspected the worst: nothing is ever finished. Meanwhile, the page itself had gotten bigger and whiter, and more forbidding. Sitting down to write, one regarded it with alarm. It glared like a searchbeam. More and more courage was required to face it.

Yet where was this courage to come from? The fiction program was better at rapping knuckles than encouraging the wild leap. If you chose to jump off a rooftop with wax wings or creep along the ground in baby steps crying, "Mother, may I?" no one would stop you. No opinions were offered on this. Discussion was restricted to the technical position of your feet on the ledge, and the paraffin density of the wings, and the exact velocity of the baby steps. If you crashed on the sidewalk, though, a circle of colleagues might appear to analyze the mess. So it was easier to creep; there was less distance to fall.

"Courage" is from the word for heart. School had little to do with heart, and everything to do with technical perfection.

How we learn is what we learn.

While the private act of the writing program may or may not be writing, the defining weekly ritual is public scrutiny. It doesn't matter whether it's your work that's up for discussion or someone else's: what is heard is criticism, what is said is criticism, until, for many, as they sit before their typewriters at home, what occupies their minds is criticism, criticism devouring their latent words.

Eudora Welty says, "I believe if I stopped to wonder what So-and-so would think, or what I'd feel like if this were read by a stranger, I would be paralyzed." And Joan Didion says, "When I first started to write pieces, I would try to write to a reader other than myself. I always failed. I would freeze up."

Yet at the Workshop we were trained to wonder all about So-and-so; we learned to write always to a reader other than ourselves. Once a week for two years we sat across a table with a Xeroxed story between us. It was tempting to write stories like a suit of armor: hollow, but impervious to attack.

And yet many of us became writers at Iowa. It was here that we noticed the nature of words.

It is possible to write for many years and never notice. It is possible to write so much one's pages swarm, and still not detect how an individual word behaves. Writing school changes that. It taps its pencil against each particular word and says, "See this." Focusing on particular words can feel niggling. It can feel pedantic, even willfully obtuse—as if the viewer insisted on standing too close to a pointillist canvas and then complained that all she saw was dots. Where are the promised sunbathers, the river, the boats? Well, if you'll just take a step back, if you'll just squint. *Squint? Step back?* The audience stares, granite-faced. No, the text must convey itself from here. When I read, I read one word at a time.

So, faced with a table of granite readers, you look at your words again. The same scene might be described in another way entirely. You might ax all the adjectives, like chipping barnacles from the sleek prow of a ship. You might shift the whole thing into interior monologue and allow adjectives to bloom like cabbage roses, saturating the telling with the deep color of emotion. If you can change anything, you can change everything. A gulf appears; you have lived on a fault line and never noticed it. Now it has broken open, leaving you over here, and what you wrote over there. Forever after, this is how it shall be.

No longer can you assume, as I did, that the way you feel writing something will be pretty much the way a person will feel reading it. I used to go to a diner under the Number 1 elevated train, and order a grilled corn muffin and jelly, and many cups of coffee, and I wrote in a sort of pounding exaltation. I assumed my readers would experience a similar thrill. The method was to get very, very excited. The story was just the conduit to convey this excitement. The writing was the same as my jumpy fingers, or the train racheting overhead and making my heart vibrate.

Writing school detached the words from the vibration. I saw that the inchoate mood and the particular words—the heart's rattle and the lines of prose—may approach each other more and more closely, but they will never merge. You may fling a million strings of words, and lace them tight, and still there is a gap.

And then, astonished, you see something else: the reader isn't granite. It is words themselves that are stony. A sort of gritty earth-bound gravity inheres in them. It is they who are stubborn, not the reader. The reader *does* squint, *does* step back and approach and turn things every which way trying to discern the depicted shape. The reader wants a good story. It is words themselves that are reluctant to cooperate.

The workshop does have a treasure to bestow. It teaches a new way of seeing. This is a loss of innocence that opens the way to all the pleasures of consciousness. It is often beautiful to revise, to enrich one's story and focus it more clearly. Moments spring to sharp life that before lay blurry. The real purpose of the story may now reveal itself. One increases the chances for a story's success.

Yet learning to write hurt me. I had to give up a sense of natural unity with my writing—of the rightness of my intuitive way. I recall the sensation that a certain story of mine had atomized. All its parts were sprayed out in various directions and hung, unrelated to one another and divorced from me. How far away they looked! Losing trust in the instinctive aptness of one's words is a form of exile. My anger at writing school is in part due to this necessary loss, and to that extent my anger is misplaced.

The formal training needs a counterbalance. Training in caution needs training in danger. So much polish needs rawness. So much restraint needs wildness. So much head needs heart. Before there was light there was "Toehu-vavohu," to use the original Hebrew: there was a mishmash, a topsy-turviness. The earth was "unformed and void," which does not mean that the earth did not exist. It existed, but without shape. It existed unrecognizably, shrouded, wanting.

It is easier to make sense saying what has been said before— we already know how to hear what we've already heard—than saying something new. We need to make nonsense on the way to making sense. We need to allow our work to be unrecognizable, shrouded, wanting, and still know it is real.

The best art risks most deeply. It is intended not for a group of readers but for one. It descends into the subterranean, the shameful, the fraught, the urgent and covert. What could not be said aloud because it defies conversation. What could not be said aloud because it could exist only as this constellation of scenes, this concatenation of details on this page. What passes invisibly over the earth because you have not yet pointed a finger at it.

To supplement the formal workshop we need an informal one, where students are told, Write about what is most frightening to write. Write what makes you feel guiltiest. Write about the most passionate you ever have been. Write images, a whole string of images you do not understand. An ear full of earwax that you scoop with your finger and it turns out to be a contact lens. A house you left where someone lies dead. You have to go back and bury them. Your husband digs a big trench in the backyard. You are worried the landlady will see.

Write about the time you were so sick you heard sirens although there were none, or the time you were so healthy for so many dull sane days you wished you were sick. Write what you are afraid will be sentimental, boring, melodramatic, pornographic, derivative, trite, vulgar, indulgent, sick, and/or stupid. There are a hundred reasons not to write what you most want to. Fuck that. Write it anyway.

We should be told: Write fast, write close to the bone, write for ten hours straight until you're not thinking in words anymore but in colors, in smells, in waves of memory. Write what you care about. Don't write one more word you don't care about. Don't waste any more of your life on what does not matter to you. Write only what matters to you—those scenes, those dialogues. Get messy. Before you get neat, get very, very messy. Write until you are more alive than you have ever been before.

So many of us were good in school, and we wanted to be good in school some more. We needed someone to say, Don't be good in school anymore. Be done with school. Be in school, but be done with school. Writing teaches writing. Your writing will teach you how to write if you work hard enough and have enough faith.

How to learn faith? My friends taught me. I saw how they lived, and it made my own way possible.

Imagine a page of text with a gigantic margin. The brief typeset part is the formal workshop. The margin, swirling with various scenes in croissant shops and bars and bedrooms and apple orchards, is the rest of the life of the place, where I learned much, unexpectedly, uniquely, implicitly. Certain scenes from it belong to me like objects:

Sitting on Gary's second-floor back porch beside the yellow torrents of willow leaves shining in the dusk lamps. We reclined in rusty lawn chairs while he read aloud from a children's book he was writing called, I think, *Families Under the Sea*.

Mary grinding coffee beans in a giant corn grinder riveted to a table which I had to press down on with all my might so it didn't shimmy away. After the coffee was brewed and cut with cream, she read me William Carlos Williams, leaping up when she heard an odd sound. It was goats. They filled the back garden, chewing the tops off the red geraniums. We laughed because it was like some dumb TV show—"Please Don't Eat the Daisies"?—laughed amid those miles of sunlight careening down. Mary said the goats had leaped loose because of William Carlos Williams. Williams was in the air and they had to jump free.

Going to a party at Indira's—there were parties every weekend—where the music was thrillingly loud, and we all knew everyone, and these were all people I admired, all people who loved the same things. It was dark and smelled of cold beer and early spring, and nearly everyone was dancing.

My neighbor Susanna and I being invited to Margie's farm to read sex scenes from our work. When we arrived lentil soup was simmering on the wood stove, and there was buttery corn bread and a green salad with tahini dressing, and red wine. We scarfed up great hunks of bread, and plate after plate of soup, and when evening shrank the room into a little glowing bowl, we read. We bent toward one another around the small wood table, and candlelight flickered on each reader's face, and I knew, listening and reading and then listening again, that I was one of the privileged of the earth.

Olga Broumas visiting Iowa, and after her talk I asked her a question I had wanted to ask someone for years: "How do you endure the long times when you cannot write?" She said in that room full of writers and readers, "Even when I cannot write, I know I am still a writer, just the way I know I am still sexual even if I have not had a lover for many months."

I have thought of her answer many times over the years. It is the sort of thing that I imagine it is possible to hear—or to hear personally, transformatively—only in a place dedicated to writing.

*   *   *

When I went to school mattered. Everyone had read *Will You Please Be Quiet, Please* and thought understatement could accomplish all that was worth accomplishing. We could all be quiet, please, and we were.

My mistake was to believe this way of writing was *the* way to write. It is the mistake of the diligent student: to grasp for rules, to confuse the values of the moment with the values of all time, to want to please. "There is no hierarchy in learning," Krishnamurti says. "Authority denies learning and a follower will never learn." Or, as Lao-tzu puts it, "When they lose their sense of awe / people turn to religion. / When they no longer trust themselves, / they begin to depend on authority."

Many people are enraged at what they find when they come to writing programs. Why do teachers so often slight their students? Why do they give so little of their time? The teachers are writers, and their first loyalty is usually to their own writing.

Students come expecting to find a true mentor, someone who cares about their own writing with much of the fervor with which they care about it themselves. Some people find this guide, it's true. One friend was told, "Race your horse up a crystal mountain." This image spoke to her in her own language, and has inspired her to try for the heights ever since. Another writer was invited to meet time and again with her teacher, an *Esquire* editor, to go over drafts of her story. In the last class, the editor announced that he was publishing her story in his magazine.

For many, though, the mentor does not appear, at least not from the ranks of the writing faculty.

Jane Gallop, a literary critic, writes, "One morning while I was reading Freud, I realized that what I wanted from analysis was to understand everything enigmatic about me, what my dreams mean, why I was so afraid of fishbones and of diving into water. I realized that when I read Freud (but not Lacan) I got the impression that all this could, someday, be understood . . . I saw myself expressing various forms of psychoanalyst-envy . . . I believed psychoanalysis knew, and that if I were analyzed, or better yet if I became an analyst (my analysis was started under the guise of a training analysis), then I would get 'it.'"

I believed writing school had "it" and that by my going to writing school, "it" would be transferred to me. I thought school would make me a writer, and then thought school had failed me when it did not. But how contradictory this is! For of course at the same time that I craved the transformation from without, I would have been alarmed by any attempt to transform me, since in fact I wanted what most of us want: not to become someone else, but to find endorsement for who we already are; not to be told, "This is how to write," but to be told, "Yes, you are writing."

I read part of this essay to a friend, who told me, "But that is precisely what your first teacher said to you, only you didn't hear."

"Where? Where?" I asked, flipping through the pages.

"Well, when she said, 'Every writer has a book they do not publish. This will be yours.' She said you were a writer. She predicted you would publish books."

I nodded, abashed. For all I knew the message had been many places. Perhaps I heard only what I'd listened for. At night, wanting silence, I hear only the creak of my neighbor's foot over my head, or the poised absence of the creak before the creak occurs. I do not hear the reassuring silence washing all around me, although I wish for it with all my might. Thinking of her apartment, I hardly inhabit my own. Waiting for my words to establish something, assuming I would know exactly how I would feel when they had established that thing (I would feel established, good), I missed the clear signs.

My very first teacher, who I had regarded with such fury because she denied me, in fact gave me what I asked for. She merely assumed it was something I already possessed.

And yet, five minutes is still five minutes. I was right to expect more. That teacher had come to writing late, after her many children were grown. I suppose she felt that the time she had left she must hoard for herself, and that her heart had already been consumed by too many others.

In the first writing class I ever took, at the New School for Social Research, a woman sat in front of me. Her body was crooked—she was a dancer who'd fallen onstage. She wedged a book under one buttock so she could sit up straight. It was always the same book: a paperback with an electric pink cover and a title I did not understand, *If You Meet the Buddha on the Road, Kill Him!* Why kill the Buddha? Why not embrace the Buddha, follow the Buddha, cherish him? I longed for Buddhas, their compassionate eyes and knowing half-smile, the sense that they could see me through and through like gazing to the leafy bottom of a lake. I longed to deliver myself up to a Buddha.

But being brushed off is the lesson. Worshipping another is not useful; desire for approval leads the artist astray. My Buddha pushed me away from her. I had read all her books the summer before, and I thought, If only I can meet the woman who wrote these sentences! If only the writer who conceived these scenes would be unfolded to me! In pushing me away from her, she pushed me toward my own self. I didn't like this. I was too full of questions. I'd come here for answers. I wanted to be different by the time I left. I wanted to make contact with the Buddha in her, but she needed every last bit of her Buddha for herself, and I was forced to discover my own way.

THE WILD YELLOW CIRCLING BEAST: WRITING FROM THE INSIDE

M Y WHOLE LIFE I HAVE ALWAYS felt the most myself when I was alone, and when I was a child there were just two places where I could go to be alone. One was the bathroom, which got tedious fast, and the other was the orange chair. The orange chair was a perfect half-sphere, padded all around. I'd push it right up flush against the sill of the living room window, climb aboard like hoisting into a dinghy, and then swirl the thick, heavy curtains so they draped behind me. I was in a tiny room.

It was enough just to be there, but most of the time I'd eat something pleasant, like a mound of strawberry ice cream in a Pyrex dish or a handful of raisins. And I'd read: Dickens's *Christmas Carol* in stiff blue leatherette, the pages jammed with tiny type; *Island of the Blue Dolphins*, all about a girl stranded on a tropical island and what she did each day; and *To Kill a Mockingbird*, twice. Heat from the radiator poured at my feet. Below me, when I gazed out, was the static picture of the garden with its box elder tree, the red brick wall of the apartments perpendicular to ours, children playing on the pavement, and usually a lady pushing her wagon full of shopping. Through the shut glass they looked far away. I was in a small quiet pocket separate from them and from my cacophonous family, and the flame inside me could grow brighter here, swelling in a cup of air. Words conjured things. The story of a Southern girl seeing snow for the first time made me happier than I had ever been before.

Writing my second novel was like sitting in that place. How glorious I felt! I wrote, sometimes, in a rapture. I induced a heady reverie. Sometimes I left my desk to dance to Sting, the same echoey song over and over again. Sometimes I stared up from my pages, breathing fast through my mouth. Of course there were days the story ran dry. It slipped into the earth before me, and I stood stumped. Usually, though, words came in a rush, and I set them down almost carelessly. There was someone I read to, a quiet blond Vermont woman who poured me tea from her grand-mother's rose china teapot and served cookies on a silver tray. Overlooking the descending mountainside, she told me how good my words were, and I drove away thrilled. That time of my life was like sitting in that secret space. The horror of it hit me when I took some pages to Long Island, and read them to another friend.

"It indulges itself," he said, gently. "It's full of authorial speeches and heightened language. It's like a boat that pulls a foot from the shore and unfurls all its sails. Get more scene going first. You need to show us a whole lot more."

Hot pins pricked my body, and then the sensation was over. It was a perfect early summer afternoon: blue sky, green grass. The lightest of breezes blew on our bare arms. My papers felt like a horrible mass in my hands. I watched an ant crawl up the side of my Adirondack chair. It curved over the armrest and began to crawl toward my elbow. He was right. I knew my friend was right. Through all that afternoon and evening (we walked on the beach, ate a supper he prepared, watched a dumb movie on TV) I knew my friend was right, and all night long I knew it too. Morning came, and I waited for the railroad. My friend kissed my cheek before I left and murmured, "Everything will be fine." I didn't believe him. How could I believe him? I'd loaded one bas-ket full of all my eggs. The basket was heavy with eggs but still, unreasonably, gloating, merry, I'd loaded them.

The train stopped often. From my window I watched people coming in. Women with precise hairdos carried impressive leather attachés. Younger women in thongs and baggy shorts blew kisses to men out on the platform. I closed my eyes, but it didn't speed time. I opened them again, and read a few pages from my manuscript. Not bad, I thought. Needs work, but even so. There's something here. There's something that can certainly be brought out. The railroad tilted straight toward Manhattan, at long last picking up speed, and it carried me shrieking and flying and thrumming like one long engine into the midst of a wordless summer.

What happened to me happens to many. It touches on a central paradox. On the one hand, we must write for ourselves. On the other, we must not forget the world. We must sit in our nook, our mental nook, the curtain around us in a space private as any voting booth or photographer's cloaked crouch, and yet imagine always the needs of the audience. I'd forgotten my audience. I assumed my needs were the reader's needs, and often they were not. "Writing is like something you do in a dark room," Frank Conroy once said. My friend turned on the light for me, and I saw what I had done. Of course, it wasn't as bad as I thought. Nor was it as good.

I was writing those days on a yellow lined pad which said DARTMOUTH in bold black letters across the top, although I was not then affiliated with the school. The pages were so satiny they seemed laminated. I flipped them over and wrote on the paler, porous side. I used a large flat handwriting that reminded me of my sister's handwriting when she was younger; it was a handwriting like practical brown Thom McAn shoes. It stood its ground placidly, unbudgingly, with a sort of oblivious dogmatism. When I had filled twenty-five or thirty pages with this handwriting I knew I had finished a chapter. Sometimes, though, I didn't know what came next, and then I resorted to another kind of handwriting. This kind of handwriting I had learned in a dream. In the dream my friend Sasha showed me where she wrote. On her desk were pages of normal, legible handwriting. Pinned to her bulletin board, though, were little pages filled with small, energetic, fluid handwriting.

"What's this?" I asked.

"Oh, that's just tiny print writing," she said.

When she wrote in tiny print writing, I could see, she felt all sorts of freedoms, and reams of scenes and dialogues spawned in her mind, and she wrote swiftly. When she was done, rich work covered the page.

"Tiny print writing looks wonderful," I said, enviously.

She said, "But I learned it from you."

This was the second dream I'd had in which I envied another writer, and through envy learned something I yearned to know. The envy acted as a boomerang, carrying me far away, only, with a *ping* like the snap of a rubber band or the Zen *klopf* that startles one into enlightenment, to return me with a gasp to myself. In the first dream a writer I knew named Leon had published three novels out of a planned series of five. He was in a bookshop signing his latest book. I pulled a copy off the shelf and discovered that he had written all about childhood. Envy parched my mouth and made my body hollow, and my hand became so weak it could scarcely support the book. I myself longed to write about childhood, and was even in fact writing about it just then—my own novel was actually centered in childhood—and yet I always felt it was an illegitimate thing to write about; it was indulgent.

I suspected there was something wrong with me, that I suffered from an arrested development. The only page I cared for in *A Portrait of the Artist as a Young Man* was the very first, about the moocow coming down along the road, and baby tuckoo, and the wild rose blossoms on the little green place. The lines from this first page came to me often, in fact, weaving through my mind like a poem you can't quite understand, like Baudelaire's "La Vie Anterieure" ("The Former Life"): "Long years I lived under vast porticoes / That thousand fires of ocean suns stained bright . . . " In his *Portrait*, though, Joyce did not linger on the distorted perceptions of early childhood, but moved on briskly to depictions of boyhood and, before you knew it, manhood, because after all it is chiefly adults who interest adults.

Similarly, the only part I recalled years after reading *The Education of Henry Adams* was about how "the children knew the taste of everything they saw or touched, from pennyroyal and flagroot to the shell of a pignut and the letters of a spelling-book—the taste of A-B, AB, suddenly revived on the boy's tongue sixty years afterwards." Five hundred and five pages of wavery archaic type about John Hay and William Henry Seward and William Ewart Gladstone printed as if even the publisher couldn't decide if this book were a curio or precious scripture— and still that phrase on page 8 was the entire residue of the thing in my mind: "the taste of A-B, AB." I thought of that phrase a lot, in fact, wishing I could taste A-B, AB myself, and at the same time criticizing myself with the thought that that great figure, Henry Adams, also fled from childhood with a sort of dismissive, appalled haste, as if the goo of irrationality might taint him if he lingered, as if the edifice of intellect were established on a swamp, and it was better to pay as little attention to the swamp as possible, lest it begin to fascinate.

And so in my dream when I saw Leon's book about childhood I was struck with envy—that he could value what he valued, that he could allow himself to be entranced by what entranced him. In the passage I read, a boy pedaled a tricycle down a slate walkway. I recognized that walkway. It ran up to a gray house my family inhabited one timeless summer. A table stood in the living room of that house. Every time I thought of this house I thought of this table. It was round cherrywood, with drawers like quadrants of pie, and when you pulled the handles the drawers revealed pastel-colored ceramic figurines—a pink pig, a gray cat, a yellow rooster, a grinning red-haired girl in a light blue jumper, a sailor like Cracker Jack hoisting a curve-bottomed green sack over his shoulder. Stories emanated from these figures, were inseparable from them. Any arrangement you put them in immediately suggested events—who did what to whom, and what happened next. My mother frowned on my brother Kenny and me going into the marvelous drawers and playing with the ceramics. But I couldn't resist. How peculiar they were! When you shoved the drawer closed hard, they rumbled as if doing a secret, thunderous dance.

So Leon had inherited my legacy of stories. The secret compartment had become his. And the slate of the pathway was the slate my brother and I wrote on in chalk. Large flat ovals in the grass: they took the white chalk like a blackboard, and the letters lasted until the next rain. This path of writing was now Leon's. How had I ceded all this to him? I woke up envying him his conviction that writing about childhood was important, and then realized that if I could admire him in this way, I knew it was important too.

Envy had a gift for me. It was green on one side, but gold on the other. The vice that had so dissipated my days, that had so often dug in its chigger-heels and devoured me, now showed itself to be a boon. For what I could not feel directly myself, I could come close to, I could approximate, through envy. Envy had placed a scepter in my hands, and although it was spiked on one end, with the other it allowed me to touch what I most desired. It was possible for someone to feel what I wanted to feel. If someone else could feel it, then I could learn to feel it too. Every character in your dreams is you, they say. In what compartment of myself did Leon reside?

I copied from my dreams. Their methods became mine. Little print writing rushed over my pages; the mood of childhood saturated the room, and its distortions, its shadows and its bogeymen, allowed me to see what I could have understood no other way. I took to writing on smaller slips of paper, yellow legal pages folded once, twice, then ripped into rectangles with edges soft as a ragged-edged book and folded in half again.

It was as if I were writing secrets. It was as if I were writing details to be read and swallowed at once, like the ciphers of a spy. I had at last outwitted the part of me that wanted everything I did to count, everything I did to prove something about me I had not yet managed to prove. DARTMOUTH, it said across the dark green band on top of the pad, like some headline proclaiming THIS IS CEREBRAL. THIS IS OF CONSIDERABLE IMPORTANCE. And I flipped the pages over and tore them to bits, and wrote where the paper drank the ink freely, in a script that reminded me of hidden intimacies—a note on the sealed inner lip of an envelope, a remark in the margin of galleys sent from one editor to another, and dashed off in the sky blue pencil invisible to cameras and Xerox machines.

I did not plan my course. I did not know what the overall shape would be. I'd had a map—a plot outline—but soon the story I was telling did not match the plan, the views were not the same. So I folded the map and studied the signs the place itself gave—where the lushest moss grew, the direction of meander of a tidal creek—trying to find the interior's own rhythm. Plot joined the expedition unwooed, as a necessary companion. It was not the scout. The scout was a certain mood. I followed that mood, and let the shape of the story flow from that.

I wrote about totemic objects because the mood had solidified in them; my sister's white lipstick, her white Formica desk, her sealing wax which came in sticks that burned fast, burgundy red or navy blue sticks shrinking in her hand while a seam of black raced upward—carbon—and a molten pool dripped in dollops on the page. She embossed it right away, holding the imprint firm a long time, like a tourniquet. I wrote about the sister-sister dresses we had growing up, puff sleeves like pineapples, blue or yellow cotton sturdy as burlap, tied at the waist with a strip of fabric so that the belt loops stuck out all around. Not twins—six years separated us—we matched like hollow dolls where the larger swallows the smaller. We wore our hair the same: cut straight across the forehead, clasped in back with a ponytail holder like two sourballs. We sat for hours side by side, caressing each other's arms. The hinge of her inner elbow astonished me: stippled, a bruised violet and pink, it was the softest thing I'd ever touched. Our real names were a matching set—Anita, Bonita—forming our own little alphabet. "Sisters should love each other" was my mother's favorite phrase. She'd been glad I was a girl so that my sister and I would always have each other. She herself had had no sister, and I think she felt unknown in the world. Our eyes would be mirrors for each other, my mother had assumed, but when I found myself in my sister's lofty eyes I was a tiny, shrunken thing that could be flicked away at a glance, while in my eyes she assumed heroic stature, her proportions enormous, pressing into the sky.

I wrote imbued with the mood I wanted. The mood was what I wanted to convey. The rest—the particular events, the furniture, even the characters—were embodiments of the mood. It was the mood that still overshadowed me; it was the mood I did not understand, and which remained compelling—as if a country I'd once visited had now vanished, as if the taste and mood of A-B, AB was something I must recreate and apprehend. I had lived in that mood for an epoch of my life, like clothes I could not pull off, a hand that would not let go of me. In my room with a door that shut behind me, and yellow pages full of tiny writing everywhere, it was the mood that was most alive. It was a beast I entered when I entered the room. It was a yellow rushing circling beast I stepped into and became.

I did not know the shape of what I wrote. I was afraid to know its shape too soon. Because then it might resemble something in the world already, and I thought my novel should be something new since nobody had yet lived my life. I did not want to truncate or stretch my story to resemble the shape I supposed it should be rather than the shape it was. A thought about something kidnaps the truth of it—the unique experience of it—so that it resembles something that's been thought before. Thoughts resemble thoughts. They fold into one another, disappear into one another, so that a new thing, abstracted enough, looks exactly like something else. "Oh, yeah," we say. "It's really just that same old thing," which by now it has almost become.

I am tracking how I came to write what my friend found wanting, and which in fact *was* wanting. It was not coherent yet. I'd lit out in one long foray toward meaning. Because at a certain point it is necessary to abandon overt meaning, the arrangement of sentences that no longer corresponds to what you have inside you. We must strike out toward what we only can *feel* we mean. After all, why write if not to heal the rift between the hours we have lived through and the authoritarian grid of language?

In a Spanish literature course I took in graduate school, there were many people who spoke a nuanced, Chilean Spanish. My own tongue was a swollen, lazy thing in my mouth when I spoke Spanish, and my ideas contracted and contracted until they parodied themselves. For every four English words, there is only one in Spanish, and often I didn't know it. When I spoke, my words were dense wood blocks I must arduously line up. If I was excited, it was worse.

Yet even in our native language, words are often dictatorial, stiff, coercive. We chop our meaning down to size. Something in us froths, pants, beds down in bewildered loneliness.

I once went to a psychologist who handed everything back to me in such reasonable terms that my unease only increased. It was as if she had a plot, a narrative line, that she applied to me like a dress pattern. Whatever didn't fit was my neurosis, and ought to be snipped. I felt she matched me to a textbook, she listened for what I said that resembled a personality profile she'd studied—a profile like the identical silhouettes at the start of "To Tell the Truth" when we grew up, swallowing up the individual contestants. I did not know what was wrong with me. That was why I came.

She listened, though, with a purpose of her own; she listened for some things and not for others, when it might have been precisely these other things that were most lonely, that most needed to be heard. And she was skeptical of my passions, as if I was making things up, as perhaps my psyche was, but for a *reason*. Everything has its story, even—especially—those things we do not understand. I recall standing in the blank sunlight on the pavement outside her office after a session, wanting to believe in the simple, pragmatic vocabulary she used, wanting it to console, while the part of me that had still never been heard raced within me, frantic, like mice in the walls. Go away, I thought. I refuse to keep making you up! And, indeed, as I walked numbness crept over me, a familiar depression, as if the worst had been confirmed.

How was it that she spoke? In clear, balanced sentences. With a firm assurance that was almost pompous, just the slightest bit obtuse. It reminded me of my own handwriting when it is like practical brown Thom McAn shoes, stolid and round, unbudging on the page. It was like the voice of a schoolteacher with a neat bow at her collar, who looks just over the heads of her pupils, seeing none of them so that she might see them all.

In an odd reversal, she typified the solipsistic narrator, shut in her muffled office, screened by a receptionist, sitting lumpish in her chair beside a plant with four leaves that like some strange emblem formed a square, and wearing large heels and a stiff cotton blue blazer and skirt. She was like a narrator who determined her plot from the outset, and could only chastise her erratic characters. She was the favored therapist of everyone in the Iowa Writers' Workshop, her name passed hand to hand like a charm, and yet she presided over a static realm, the light so filtered through the tilted blinds that it was just a warm gray, like the sedative air of a dentist's. Her response to fear was rigid, droll calmness. The tissues at one's elbow in their hard white plastic box seemed both prompt and castigation; a crust of dust had settled over them. They jutted stiff as tulle beside the mahogany lamp and the clock whose face forever held secret communion with the therapist.

Yet I listened to this woman with dire attention. It seemed I would heal myself insofar as I approximated these most reasonable words. In my chair opposite her big framed doctoral degree, sitting beneath the wall of thick, official-looking volumes, I felt quite sick, like an erratic, bizarre person, although on the street, or with my friends and students, I felt normal, merely going through an unhappy time.

To be honest, I envied her words, I envied her ability to see the world reasonably. The reasonable way of seeing the world lopped off all the un-uniform parts, to me. When you cut cookies with a cookie cutter, peripheral scallops emerge as you press down, little jutting jigsaw-puzzle pieces like the spokes of a daffodil. You line up the even, round cookies on the lightly greased sheet, and then lift up all the scallops and fronds and doily-curls, all the edible filigree, mold it firmly into a ball, and then cut uniform cookies from that. It takes a lot of effort, it takes a lot of conscious concern and patience to set rows of pretty, perfectly round incised circles one after another on the sheet. I saw my sister do it many times, her careful, neat fingers encouraging the floured circles to shimmy off the spatula without stretching, the final display of disks on tinfoil a triumph of mastery. I couldn't do it. My cookies ended grubby with thumbprints and pinching, distended and abrupt. I drew them from the oven with dismay. I both admired and feared those who could achieve formal success, who when they spoke spoke clearly if unextraordinarily, and who obviously felt what they said matched what they meant like two sides of a snap snapping together.

I meant to achieve a form that was successful, but eventually. I would delve into my subject, into my mood, and then later, if I had to, deal with the form of the novel. Perhaps distortions aren't distortions if the canvas is sufficiently ample, or the right shape. Perhaps if you continue along stoked by enough faith, a sort of pattern will emerge like the pattern of DNA, inherent, integral to the essence of the thing. When I was a child we would take a piece of paper and set it over the embossed title of a book, then take a pencil and rub it along its length to watch the title swim up, *David Copperfield* or *Martian Chronicles* appearing on the blank page like fate.

And yet, what feels coherent from the inside, from the outside often does not make sense. What a hard truth this is! Most writers have broken their hearts against it. What feels so clear the writer blushes to explain—*there it is, right there on the page*—might elude the reader entirely, who squints, sighs, and finally claps the book shut. And the disjointed narrative sounds schizoid; and the associative novel lazy and unedited—and it's not just Uncle Mel who thinks so, but the best readers you can get. Well, then, something's the matter, something's deeply the matter, even though the heart rankles: "I spoke to you in the language of truth, and you don't understand!"

At The Wail Coffeehouse in Beverly, Massachusetts, a woman with coursing blond hair and a fabric-covered book mounted the stage. "I wrote this poem this afternoon," she said. "I hope I can read it before my throat closes up." It was about loneliness, and lying in her bed at night feeling her heart pounding within her. She read it in a soft, breathy voice, and when she was done she looked up. We applauded politely. She blinked, then rose stiffly, as if her stomach were full of splintered glass, the disappointment palpable about her as she returned to her folding chair. Watching her I thought, I hope to God I'm different, although I suspected I was not. The chief difference between us was that I wrote and rewrote, and that I read and reread, and that I hadn't dared a poem in over a decade. Our hopes were exactly the same.

If only the spontaneous were always perfect! If only what felt forceful when written always delivered itself forcefully when read! We travel along, scarcely knowing. Even from the lookout, we're often blind. Australia was discovered when a ship smashed right into it. Form struck out of the haze of sea and air that enclosed the travelers. They took out their pen and paper and redrew the world.

My Australia came the day my friend said that my novel indulged itself. Instead of presenting scenes that let the reader experience the characters' predicament, I told about it using language I hoped conveyed its importance. And the scenes I had written hung like stars in a constellation not yet named, a shape still unseen. No chapter began: "So, the next day . . ." A year might have passed between one chapter and the next. The point-of-view might have changed.

Sometimes, with a laugh between pride and despair, I would say I was writing a book like a honeypot ant. This kind of ant, I'd discovered, hangs in the colony's storage place and is fed on honey. Its body swells into a golden sphere bound by the thin black lines of the ant's skeleton. It looks like a lit basketball or a globe of stained glass. When the colony needs honey, the other ants suck it from the live stored ant. I imagined my book as being something like this, a thing with a prefab structure, the anatomy of chapters in a row, into which lots of interesting stuff could be put. I didn't have to understand in advance how each new section fit with the rest. If I sensed that it pertained, if it was lit by the same mood, I harvested the honey and stuffed it in. Let it be a great big book, I thought. Let it have a lot of life crammed into it.

"Have you been writing on your book?" my friend Mary asked, as if I was chewing on a big piece of barbecue.

"Oh, yes," I'd say.

It was pleasant not knowing what the book would amount to. When I wrote stories I knew where they were headed. They were jaunts, without much time to explore. I'd embarked on a novel to see what was over the horizon. I sailed off into the haze. In the indeterminate atmosphere I nosed along pleasurably, until Australia hauled up and smashed me flat.

* * *

My friend and I walked along a pier on Long Island. It was
the morning after he'd informed me of the demands of novelistic
form to which I'd acted oblivious and which had therefore dissipated my force.

"Can you think of a way the book *might* work?" I asked, kick-
ing a chunk of stone along the boardwalk. My friend was a fine
writer. He already had a novel published. "Can you imagine some
way I could write the book I mean to?"

"Well," he said, pondering. "Sure. It could go like this. You
could start with a scene where the sisters are adults. The younger
one is really nasty toward the older one. The reader will wonder
what's going on. Have you ever read *Ethan Frome?* It opens with
two old women speaking very bitterly to a man. You immediately
wonder who they are and what's happened. Then Wharton goes
back in time and builds up to how they ended like that."

I nodded. That made sense.

"After that, the first seventy-five pages or so could be about
childhood. And then the next hundred and fifty pages could be
the characters' current situation as adults, when the older comes
to live with the younger again."

It could work! Why, he even had the number of pages for
each section figured out.

The air was filled with the clang of rigging against aluminum
masts, the soft clear ringing that sounds at once close and far
away. A few sailboats were out, gliding along in the distance as if
pulled on a thread, though if you were out there the wind would
be beating the taut sails and your face would sting with salt-spray.
The boats moved very fast, bent low. By our feet the water
slopped, greenish-black. Clumps of dense, brown-podded sea-
weed thrived in the chinks. Yet how blue the water looked, far
away! The further away you looked, the bluer it was, until at the
edge of visibility you saw the Mediterranean.

I would soon be far away myself, back in the Bronx. It made
my friend's advice more important that he lived a life of such

apparent success, of strolls on the beach and Armani sweaters given by Armani himself, and supper at the homes of *New Yorker* editors because his boyfriend was famous. My visit fell a week after *The New York Times Magazine* had a full-page photo of the two men in their East Hampton living room, the sun flooding in and their faces soft-focused, handsome, as if they had some secret which made them rich and smart and happy. I was going to leave my friend in an hour, and I wanted to make sure I understood exactly what he meant.

While he was talking about the proposed novel, I nodded eagerly—yes, yes!—but as soon as he stopped I no longer understood. While he spoke I could follow the logic of his sentences, and so had the feeling I understood what they suggested, but as soon as he fell silent, I felt no reverberation within me. I did not see the scenes. I asked him to say it over, and he said it over. I asked him to explain it more particularly, and he did. It was on the verge of becoming clear.

I told myself that I would understand his idea on the train home. But on the train home I did not understand it, and I did not understand it at my desk, and I did not understand it in my dreams. I dreamed I stepped out on a stage and opened my mouth, but forgot the lines my friend had given me. I sweated and shook, but there was nothing inside.

That summer was the first summer that was apocalyptically hot, the summer when everyone not only knew what the greenhouse effect was, but believed it was true. That summer also, syringes washed ashore on Jones Beach. The ocean itself had to be quarantined. At that same time AIDS ascended at last with definitive force into the public consciousness like something dreamed up and repressed, but real. Stickers appeared on lampposts, in bathrooms of fancy restaurants, on the baskets of the tollbooths at all the portals to the city: a black circle with a pink triangle and the words SILENCE = DEATH. Horrible things were happening, *really* happening. I sat in a stupor at the desk in my parents' apartment in the Bronx. My husband's job brought us to the city, and we saved money by living here. I'd always been able to write here. But this summer was different. I gazed up at the muffled white ash of the sky, unable to think of words that were appropriate, unable to imagine how my book might go, trying to blot out the pervasive sense of futility that seemed to consolidate in the headlines every night, knowing, *knowing*, that SILENCE = DEATH, but unable to break the silence because I had broken faith with something in me.

I no longer believed something I once believed. The city, so big, so oceanic, so superlatively organized with its system of two hundred and five numbered streets against a grid of twelve named avenues—the city spoke to itself in a language it understood, in black, definitive letters in news boxes on street corners, in official, detached voices over the airwaves, and everything it said seemed more important than anything I could say. What could I be to it?

The city itself became an incarnation of my smart, voracious sister; my certified, categorical psychotherapist; even the many white-pillared universities (Dartmouth, Iowa) that seemed to hold themselves aloof, as if concentrating within themselves all that was reputably meaningful. It came to embody the part of me, in fact, that disbelieved itself. This part did not believe I made sense, and stood a ways off, observing, pretending to withhold judgment but not really withholding it, for the very stance was a judgment, the very crossed arms and scrutinizing gaze as I stood off in the doorway regarding myself.

Not an easy word, not an unforced line, that entire summer. Fetching the mail one day, I locked myself out. In a coffee shop where the waitress loaned me a pen, with my slippered feet tucked under my chair, on the back of a place mat picturing dancing Rob Roys and pink ladies sporting parasols, I wrote a letter to a friend. It was the best thing I wrote all summer long.

Not until I regained the suspension of judgment that comes

with immersion could I write again. I had to leave the apartment
where I grew up, the city where I no longer made sense, the plot
outline that did not help me get to what I meant.

My friend's advice was good advice, and yet it silenced me. If
the best advice injures you, then where do you turn? To silence?
To bad advice? My friend could not chart my story for me
because I hadn't really discovered the story yet. I'd explained to
him my idea for the story. I'd given him an abstraction, and he'd
organized it.

The story I wanted to write was still held in a big yellow pow-
derpuff clumped with Jean Naté powder, and my sister glowing
pink, emerging from the bathroom in a burst of hot air. It was
still held in the exact mucilage gold of the gum that bound her
address labels (those tiny volumes narrow as shirt seams, proclaiming on every page Anita's name, Anita's place) and in the
four-ring binder of her Harris's *Standard World Stamp Album* with
its shining, jagged teeth. There was something about all this I
still needed to understand.

Snippets of the entire world were held in Anita's books. She
slept with the twin volumes of the stamp album beside her, on
the floor by her head, tucked between the bedstand and her nubbly blue slippers. The whole world seemed to be a scrapbook she
possessed, clippings and specimens for it arriving through the
mail, and pasted in place with "hinges" shaped like tiny bottle-
green glassine books. In a few months the hinges were brittle,
and if you flipped the pages of the album dozens of stamps sprang
off with a crackle of dried leaves. These all needed to be
remounted, licked afresh, and glued back. Anita never tired of it,
as if her own mouth contained the moisture of the world, necessary to keep everything in place.

But even this was not what my novel meant to say. What it
meant to say was the exact green of the paper hinges, and the
puffy chestnut-colored vinyl of the giant books, and the smell of
the Jean Naté—sweet and lemony and cloying, as Anita stepped
out of the hot bathroom. All this formed a pattern I didn't know

yet. I had not written enough of it yet to sort it out. The only way to return to writing was to return to intuition. I could not write until I separated myself from outside authority.

In New Hampshire, leaves kindled on the trees, bursting into orange and red and yellow almost with a gasp like a pilot light lighting, and they hung there the barest instant—a week, nothing—before they flung themselves to the earth. The ground flowed with colors as if a globe had been spun. Everything urged disorder. I was writing again.

Joyful occasion! Happy hour! Returning to writing is the best homecoming there is. One draws the curtain around one's semispherical chair. At last on the page are the characters you feared had gone forever. Hello, hello! Here was Stuey in a blue clip-on bowtie, Martin with his grin and birch slingshot, Anna with her Estees diet gum, her *Joy of Cooking*, her red-hot sealing wax.

I had a choice. I could choose my way or not choose my way. Nobody else's way would deliver me into my own territory. You can't get there from here. You can only get here from here. You can only get more and more fully here during the time you are lucky enough to be here.

Can someone give you a map to you? Only you can write such a map, and you might write it by feel, doing your work in pencil, and only much later inking it in. Katsushika Hokusai writes, "Looking back over the first 50 years of my career, I can find nothing that I have done that is worthwhile. At the age of 73 I have at last arrived at the point where I can perceive the true form and characteristics of birds, animals and plants. Thus my true life as an artist is just beginning."

I could not rewrite my book until I had written it. All my friend's intelligence and aesthetic sense could not help me. I wished it could. I tried to make it. But it sat like a prosthetic device on my desk, a plastic arm, a cybernetic brain. It was not within me. I had to relinquish his form, any form, to move forward. I had to choose immersion again.

It was harder to choose it the second time, to choose it consciously. I resisted choosing it, and at last the summer was gone. We must write for ourselves, but we must not forget the world. I found the world so compelling, so admirable and intimidating, that I could not regard it and remember what I meant at the same time. I could not look outward and tell the story of what was inside.

Again I closed the curtain around me, regaining the secret place so much like the chamber that registers the images of a photograph, and which must be kept dark for the picture to be captured. The ancients knew that the deepest spiritual truths come out of mystery. Their sacred places were remote Eleusian shrines where the very act of searching and then finding was holy to them. They danced their way into discovery.

THE STORY'S BODY: HOW TO GET THE MEANING IN

A MAN WALKED UP TO ME AT A PARTY recently and asked how expensive it would be to have someone write his book. He had a title, *Our Father Who Art in Heaven*, and a big idea: a man who wants to take over the world selects on the basis of genetic data a hundred women, each from a different country. He inseminates them. "Then suddenly, twenty years later—boom!—there are all these grown sons of his, and they control the world." The man leaned close. "How much do you think it would cost to have someone write that for me?"

My mind was busy trying to work out such trivial matters as how the hundred sons would gain power over each of the governments of the world, and how all of a child's care and development could be described as taking place "suddenly," when I realized that the issue here wasn't the plot. It was this man's understanding of what it is to write a novel.

Many people think what's essential to writing is a good idea. But is a novel simply an idea made flesh? And if so, what goes into composing that flesh? This man seemed to think a book happens as "suddenly" as the rearing of a child, both germinated by a bit of seed, with the actual growing of the body some simply mechanical working-out of the seminal idea. If writing is not just a matter of picking the fanciest word to convey a preconceived notion, if it's not merely knowing how to manipulate a thesaurus ("big words," my students say when I ask what they think they need to work on most in their writing; "learning more big words"), then of what does the actual work of writing consist?

I met with a man recently to discuss the first few chapters of a novel he was writing. It read like a case study, concise histories of the characters combined with analyses of their emotional states. The author was a social worker, it turned out. When I told him what his fiction needed was scene, concrete detail, and actual voices speaking on the page, he told me it bored him to write that stuff. He could do it just fine, he was sure, but he was ambitious, he had some important things to say, and he didn't see why he needed to waste his time putting in things like the color of somebody's hair or exactly what she ate for lunch.

I blushed at my insistence on physical detail, on describing on the page objects and people that the reader can actually see. It seemed almost vulgarly carnal. What a shame that fiction rises from such a base plane! I suggested to the man that perhaps he'd rather write essays (I hesitated to say sermons). He shook his head and frowned. He wanted to write fiction, he said. He seemed dismayed I was so obtuse. I was dismayed I was so obtuse too. What were we talking about?

This man, I think, wanted to enchant the reader, to set in words certain amorphous and important sensations he had experienced. Once during our conversation he leaned toward me and confessed that the central character—a child of five—was he. "George is me," he declared, an almost comic echo of Flaubert's remark, "Madame Bovary, c'est moi." He wanted to transcribe his own inchoate experience. He wanted it to become art. He felt, as many of us do, that he had a right to that. Perhaps he wanted to feel his suffering had been worthwhile, was dignified, for he did write about suffering; perhaps he wanted to feel less alone, to feel his life had been redeemed, and its true worth, the value so absent from his daily experience yet so necessary to his heart, was now realized on paper, the dross burnt off and the gold revealed.

No delight in language motivated his pen. The world's physical details were so much debris. His few scenes puddled toward ellipses, seemed uninterested in achieving "moments"—they gestured hastily toward something never glimpsed on the page, although each chapter concluded with triumphant relief, as if to say, "So there. Now that's established." It made you want to flip the page over to see if there was something you were missing. Yet he meant to write fiction; fiction was what he attempted every night. This man seemed to want the transcendent transformation that novels can achieve. He didn't know how to achieve it, though, and he wanted a shortcut. Like all of us, he was in a hurry.

That evening, my husband invented a parable. A young painter comes to Michelangelo and says, "I've seen your religious paintings. Teach me to depict the human soul."

"Fine," says Michelangelo. "Learn to paint a human knuckle. Observe the knuckle closely. See all its bones and webs of skin, and the exact way it puckers. Study its minute shifts of color. You may paint a soul only by painting a knuckle."

You may paint a soul only by painting a knuckle. You may convey terror or longing or regret or exhilaration only by giving us the color of somebody's hair and exactly what she ate for lunch, and red high heels, and an attaché case's handle stained darker by the oils of a human hand, and a skinny buck-toothed girl singing "Yes, We Have No Bananas" on a black-and-white TV, and olives, and three o'clock, and the Scotch-taped hem of a Bergdorf Goodman dress, and venetian blinds, and a woman's eyes fixed for many minutes on a scarred tabletop, and a tin spoon ringing against the side of a mug. There are no shortcuts.

When I first learned this I was outraged. Nothing had prepared me: not decades of reading, not a whole education in English literature. My high school creative writing teacher—a tall, elegant woman who fancied hats—tacked up a postcard of

T. S. Eliot the first day of class and announced that she intended to refer to him so frequently, she would, for convenience, call him simply "Tseliot." We were to know whom she meant. She told us that she'd visited Florence that summer, and enacted for us the various writhing poses of Michelangelo's captives in marble, culminating in the depiction of her rapture when she saw— at last! right before her at the end of the corridor!—the *David*, and she added what a relief it was to be teaching literature again, what a relief to be away from the mothers on park benches discussing the price of peas.

We were in a rapture. Tseliot! The *David!* This tall slim woman with the mascaraed, high-cheekboned face and a knack for conjuring a whole scene with just a lift of her hands, the widening of her eyes! We despised the price of peas! We despised mothers on park benches! We were consecrated to art, to beauty, to certain affinities of the spirit that canned vegetables couldn't in a million years so much as touch. Canned vegetables and their price, and their look—a bowl of ridged carrots steaming before one, a bowl of peas, greenish-yellow, round, dented, regular in size, legumes—*legumes!*—why the very word showed their utter cloddishness, as if each were a tiny corpse to be eaten, potatoish, stupid, yanked from the earth to yank us back into the earth—a bowl of cooked vegetables was the opposite of everything we meant.

It was affiliated with our particular and ungainly past, with mothers and aprons and mouths in need of wiping, and half-forgotten memories of ice cream melting depressingly into one's dolloped wedge of birthday cake—with, that is to say, all that left one feeling limited and helpless, all that moored one to the earth. It was affiliated, as well, with all the sights and smells of the shut apartment that in adolescence made one long for distant places, places with marvelous diphthong names: Siam, Sevilla, Tangiers, where, amidst the sweet, acrid fragrance of incense, through air that shimmered with heat, one's eyes slit like a cat's in the sensual opulence of the place, the low couches, the blue sky, the music that has woven on and on so long, so repetitively, that it has melted the iron bars of one's mind and one has slipped out . . . That steaming bowl of vegetables was affiliated with all of us that was never sufficiently understood, all of us that stood as traitors and orphans in our own homes, all that we could not say to those we loved because it would have appeared ridiculous, because it would have appeared pompous and arrogant—and chiefly because we did not know the words for what we meant.

We did not know what we meant, but we knew what we did not mean, and that was a bowl of peas. Yet there was hope! The masters pointed the way! For, just as we understood that Tseliot with his watch chain and his waxed hair had never really been an American although he was born in St. Louis; just as we understood that Michelangelo himself had put horns on Moses and yet still managed to create a figure of sublime beauty; so too we saw that with enough insight and effort we might transcend the Bronx, the banging, bargaining, barging-around Bronx full of squalling sisters and a grandmother pursuing us—actually pursuing us through the apartment!—with a bowl of Wheatena in her hands. "Essen! Essen!" she cried, and we laughed at the absurdity of it even then, but did not slow our pace.

"Transcend" was the magic word that year. When our teacher explained it, I could hardly believe that one word could mean such a marvelous, complicated thing. *Transcend*, like an invisible departure, like the ghostly white whoosh an old photo managed to register if a person moved. The important part was the blur, not the body. The important part was what you could not see. What you could see was the detritus, the fixed and fraudulent. It was like a boy sizing you up by your face. What was your face to you? Had you chosen your face? Could you exchange it for another more apt? It was a mask, a wall, a bowl of peas. Those to whom it was important were the plodders of the earth, forever deceived.

"I used to read," remarked a woman on a Greyhound bus.

She'd seen me bent over *Light in August*. "Now I crochet." I smiled and nodded. She was a pleasant woman, with bright blue eyes. She was going to visit her brother and his wife and their three boys and one girl. They lived just outside Waterbury in a lovely ranch house with a very pretty wood-chip lawn so that you never had to mow. This woman seemed quite nice, but talking to her left me breathless, gasping, as if my life were being sucked out of me. "Um-hmm," I said, and plunged back into my novel, which I read as if everything symbolized something else, as if things were arrows all pointing away, away, and nothing was what it seemed.

School taught this way of reading. It was a lesson I liked. We wrung each novel between the clenched rollers of interpretation until an ounce of pure meaning squeezed out and the plot, that old bag, could be tossed. We processed literature; we consumed it. We "learned" *The Great Gatsby, Macbeth, Pride and Prejudice* as if they were Aesop's Fables and Aesop had cleverly concealed the meaning inside Nick Carraway and Banquo and Elizabeth Bennett, as if the interpretation was superior to the poetry, as if these books had been written to be deciphered, and once a book yielded its interpretation, it could be pretty much thrown away.

"This literature course has made it easier to find the deep, hidden meaning," my college students sometimes write on evaluation forms. Occasionally they remark, "I like the way we discussed this novel's deep, hidden meaning."

"Where is it hidden?" I once cried, flipping a book upside down and shaking it. "Come on! Where's that deep old thing hidden?" I peered into the binding. I tossed the pages all about.

But my students gazed knowingly, arms crossed over chests, slight smiles on their lips, as if to say the meaning was indeed hidden in there, they were not fooled. The meaning was hidden in there because before they came to class they hadn't seen the things we talked about, and now they saw them. But it was as if they'd returned to a meadow having been tutored in wildflowers

and birds, and suddenly their eyes distinguished devil's paint-
brush and orange hawkweed and grackles and martins and gray
catbirds where before there had just been a swatch of bright blossoms and a flutter in the leaves. Are the flowers hiding less now?
Are there more birds than before?

In Florida once, a man slid up to me and murmured, "This
pond is full of alligators." I thought he was teasing; it was an
empty, disappointing hole. "Look," he said. "See that little rise in
the water over there? The thing that looks like a log? It's the
snout."

Before my eyes, an alligator coalesced. The thing that looked
like a log swelled into a definite bulge holding a surprising, glassy
eye. Behind it trailed the long corrugated paddle of the body. It
was drifting, or, rather, swimming along.

The man pointed out another mud gray alligator, this one
inert, and then I saw two alligators almost at once, which I stared
at a very long time since I'd discovered them myself and so felt
almost as if I loved them. Then, with a start, I noticed a tiny alligator three steps from our feet. It was nestled on the shore, a
baby about sixteen inches long. How meticulously it was formed,
with its bumpy little back, and with each of its little alligator legs
ending in alligator fingers stretched apart on the earth as if on a
great round belly, relaxing. It looked astonishingly like what it
was supposed to look like.

"I'm a photographer on assignment from Milano," said the
man. "I was just photographing sharks in Cuba. Would you like
to rent a canoe with me?"

We talked for a while. Little discrepancies emerged in his
story until at last I couldn't say for sure where he'd been or who
he was. Perhaps it was all true. Perhaps every word was a lie. And
yet he had taught me to see alligators. Here was the baby, three
steps away.

"No thanks about the canoe," I said. "I hope your assignment
here goes well."

He nodded, watching me coolly, with gray eyes and a half-

smile, as if to say, "Too bad. You'll regret not coming with me"—
a look so intent I hurried away.

I left him where I'd met him, gazing at the shadowy pool,
incarnating alligators for those too much in a hurry to see. I was
pleased, later, when my own students learned to distinguish what
was before them. There it was, coasting about, lolling, warming
its blood. I had not put it there, nor could I take it away. It had
come of its own accord.

When the conditions are right, live things creep up. The
author does not need to airlift them in. No need to insert a rep-
tile here, something symbolic over there. The most potent meaning arises indigenously. It looks like earth, like mud, like a log.
The more your eyes discern the particulars of the physical world
and its inhabitants, the more meaningful your work becomes.
This is the meaning that, when it's laid dormant in the sun long
enough, strikes with devouring force.

So many years of assuming we should see words as arrows
pointing away, away! But fiction is not made of ideas. Nor is it
made of emotion. It is made of words that primarily mean things.
It astonished me to discover how much Flaubert, George Orwell,
Joan Didion, John Cheever, Tolstoy, Henry James, and Charlotte
Brontë all knew of clothing fabrics.

Fiction structures an experience for the reader to live
through. That is why its force can be so great. You want your
reader to feel a certain way, you want your reader to understand
what you have been forced to understand—the insight that
eludes words but that you know in your bones. Give up trying to
explain. Fiction must convince our bodies for it to have any
chance of convincing our minds. And yet is the point of our bodies our minds? Were we given shoulders and a chest and legs and
feet just so our brains would have a pedestal? The physical pleasures of a novel exist for themselves, are a good in themselves.

Transcendence is not fleeing, not an absence, but a most
attentive *presence*. To write well we must sink into the silt of this
world.

*   *   *

The can of peas is stamped "69¢" in blurry purple, as if the number were floating up through water, or as if it were an old tattoo. Innumerable peas glisten on the wrapper, peas as green as spring grass, enclosed in blue hearts. This is Sweet Life brand Medium Tender Sweet Peas. It's a full pound. Le Sueur Very Young Small Early Peas come in a shiny silver wrapper with gold lettering. A black fleur-de-lis is the only decoration. They cost ninety-nine cents for only fifteen ounces. There is something haughty about Le Sueur's restraint; the company does not depict even a single pea. It is as if they imagine one's cook will go to the larder muttering, "Peas, peas . . . aha!" when her eye falls on the word, as if it would be unseemly to expect people to be seen with a can emblazoned with a bowl of peas. The Green Giant Company owns Le Sueur, and I suppose they know their market, which is quite a different market from that of Better Valu, Your Savings Brand, whose bowl of peas practically rises to meet you as if to say, "We got what you want." The price is a mere two for eighty-nine cents for 14.5-ounce cans.

Sitting on a park bench, watching the children in the sandbox, one might, I imagine, say many interesting things about the price of peas. Mrs. Malloy might confess with a sigh that when she's lazy and it's as hot as it is today she makes stovetop tuna-noodle mix, which the kids love but her husband, Dennis, refuses to touch (she fries *him* a veal chop; he's a fussy eater; was raised by an aunt who spoiled him, and now it's Mrs. Malloy who has to pay the price).

"Stovetop tuna-noodle mix?" asks Pearl Brinkley, scrabbling for a pencil in her pocketbook. She's nineteen, unmarried, and likes to take advice, a practice she finds reassuring. She flips over an empty envelope with a glassine window, and holds a stump of pencil poised in her hand.

"Well," says Mrs. Malloy. "It's just cooked noodles, a can of tuna, a can of mushroom soup, a can of peas."

"Sounds like something you'd eat in a bomb shelter," murmurs Lila Blair, but Pearl is the only one who laughs.

Mrs. Humphries recrosses her legs and says, "By the way, have you noticed that peas have gone up again? It's ridiculous: sixty-nine cents! A year ago right now they couldn't have been more than fifty-eight!"

Mrs. Malloy thinks, Isn't she a bit of a fool, buying the sixty-nine-cent ones. The two-for-eighty-nine are just as good and, after all, it's only to dump in with the rest.

Lila Blair says, "I can't remember when I paid less than a dollar-twenty-something for my peas," although she pays only ninety-nine cents. "I like early peas."

"Early peas?" cries Mrs. Malloy. "Early peas?" She shakes her head, frowning. "Never heard of them. You're like my Dennis: fussy."

"One ought to have standards," breathes Lila Blair, and, beneath her recipe for stovetop tuna-noodle mix, Pearl Brinkley copies this down.

What does the playground look like? What does it feel like to sit for hours on a slatted wood bench? What odors are in the air? When Mrs. Malloy's Susie dashes up and claims that Francoise, Lila Blair's daughter, *scratches*, why look at the back of her arm, she scratched *there*, like an alleycat! (and, indeed, there are three jagged marks tipped with red, puffing out from the tender white skin)—what ensues?

And what ensues when Pearl Brinkley, her pocketbook bulging with the conflicting wisdom of the streets, at last trudges up the final steps to her fifth-floor walkup, her baby with its face of a rapist (yes, she can't help thinking that! She knows she mustn't, but still those horrible blue eyes are his, everyone in her family has brown, and the slight lift of the upper lip, which she can't help seeing as a sneer, just the way he sneered at her that night. She had screamed. He said, "Oh come on, what did you think we were coming here for anyway, the *view*?" and she felt so stupid, so very stupid she almost didn't scream again)—the baby just waking up now from its nap, perhaps jostled by the stairs, and writhing its small body, and blinking its huge and now staring blue eyes (its eyes are too big, she thinks, abnormally big. She knows babies have disproportionately big eyes, but this one's eyes, she thinks, are more than disproportionate. They're wrong), and swings open at last the gray door with no name on it and not even a number, only a round steel buzzer loud as a hornet, swings open the door—into what?

Into what ecstasies of baby diapers or tumbling paperback novels, or houseplants pressing their profuse green leaves hard against the glass, or Victorian nightclothes (stiff sheer cottons she can see her skin through, heaps of yellowed lace, all picked up for next to nothing at thrift shops. She always wanted to play the Queen of Sheba as her mother said. Now, in the privacy of her own apartment, or rather the near-privacy—after all, there is the baby, watching—she can): into what environs does she emerge? Is there the stink of sour dishrags, the warm, strange odor of her own milk, the scent of musk which she's learned to burn, now that she can do as she pleases in her own small, square, impoverished domain?

Impoverished, did I say? Even that abstraction misleads: a check arrives once a month, on the third day of each month, made out to her. She waits for the postman, who is not allowed to place the envelope in her hand. It goes into the mailbox, and immediately she fishes it out, rips it open, and stares. There. "Pearl Brinkley" it says on the line, typed after the cascading, swirling words "Pay to the Order of," and the imprint of the New York State Government. It makes her think of a birth certificate or a certificate of title, something official and unassailable and her own. She deposits it at the bank teller's window with a moment's regret, even though it's instantly transformed into a discrete sum of cash she can spend however she pleases. She can spend it on Le Sueur peas if she pleases, on cherry-filled chocolates, on Chinese lanterns, Lucite photo boxes, the phone bill, baby outfits, Huggies, gauzy pink stuff to drape from the curtain rods, pastel votive candles in flavors like piña colada, avocado, chocolate, peppermint, all chosen for their color and massed on the bedstand where, late at night, amidst a wild reek, she watches them burn, each candle through the scalloped glass a dozen, each dozen through her sleepy eyes a thousand raging flames.

What that door opens on is what she is, who she is, her fantasy of herself, and her reality. And the pleasure of writing this! The sheer inventive, meticulous pleasure of describing what is, what may be!

It is the *what* that matters. The *what* is what means. Things are saturated with significance. Meaning does not have to be injected into a story like juice injected into a cooked turkey. Things themselves are translucent with meaning, like paper translucent from grease. In poor houses on the frontier where people couldn't afford glass, the windows were paper rubbed with fat. The light streamed in, as did the winter cold and the summer heat, and everything was seen in that light, the light of the paper window, just the way that now, when we think of people living with great poverty and endurance, all we need to do is imagine a paper window: meaning glows in the thing.

Here is the answer to the question, Where is the deep hidden meaning hidden, and what makes it so very deep? Meaning is trapped in the *what* of things. Meaning is held in the web of things like honey held in a comb, or a soap film held in a hoop, or a bundle of the sun's radiant energy held in the very green of chlorophyll. There is a physics of significance.

Things set close enough together exert a force. How is it that sap heaves hundreds of feet up a tree? Is there a giant heart beating at the bottom of each trunk? The hearts are everywhere at once: the very closeness of the tree's vascular walls pulls the sap. The same force accounts for how blood prevails against gravity in your own legs, and for love itself, according to my high school English teacher. This was a different one, a cynic. "Propinquity!" she declared about Romeo and Juliet, the lovers in *The*

Fantasticks, even Catherine and Heathcliff. "It's all just because of propinquity."

Propinquity explains as well the meniscus, the moon-shaped curve of water in a measuring cup or any cup. The sides of the water rise; the middle sags. It's surface tension between those walls that tugs the liquid into a hammock. Surface tension is a force so strong, in fact, that the *World Book* reports if you carefully set needles and razor blades on water they will not sink.

Writers work with surface tension; all we have are surfaces. The deep hidden meaning lurks on the surface, always. Objects, action, what was felt, what was said—these are the beakers of meaning, these are the little pots and vessels which catch the dew as it forms. The physical world, thin as the reflecting surface of water, thin as the circular wafer of sun on which the very Buddha sits—it is on this that all significance rests, like a man resting in a hammock, held snug by a web of strings.

A moment of time can be a thing too, of course, and so it also can lasso significance. A moment of time can be a thing as hard and fixed and clenched as a knot in your own back. The time your father said, "Why are you so stupid?" softly, almost nonchalantly. You looked up from the Christmas gift you were opening—already you could see it was just a gray acrylic sweater with giant argyles, wrong, all wrong, not at all what you meant when you mentioned what the other boys were wearing, why couldn't your mother see the difference or understand that it mattered? It made you sorry for her, sorry for you both, because she tried—looked up as your father set down his whiskey glass (in your memory it is just a gold blur), looked up to see your mother's face—slip. A slight slip. Something registered behind the eyes. You couldn't say what it was. It was just barely perceptible (she tried not ever to let her pain show; it was the sole source of pride she had left, and this was Christmas), and so the moment caught you. It was a thing.

Even now you could pick it up like something kept in your top-desk drawer; it was there without you needing to think about it, and you touched it lightly from time to time the way a man will half-consciously touch his wallet in the city. Was it that your father had seen the expression flick across your face when you glimpsed the argyle sweater, or was it that your mother had the liquor bottle in her hands and was going to where she always hid it under the sink, that made him call her stupid?

Maybe it was something else, something to do with how falsely cheery she was that morning, rousing you from bed early. It had been so early, in fact, that you didn't even have time to develop a feeling of expectation, a feeling that was one of the pleasures of the holiday, for you—roused you while you were still clinging to dreams. Gray light filled the corners of the room like fog. You went right to her, smiling immediately, an echo of her own smile, and went down to where the presents were, under the tree, and waited.

When your father at last arrived he was in pajamas that seemed askew and somehow grimy, and he gave your mother a look of pure something, a look that burned with pure something. Was it hatred? Sexual antagonism that had turned to bitterness? Again and again you tried to understand that look. At last you were forced to acknowledge that your very incomprehension was part of the problem, that who you were was connected to why you failed to understand your father's look, so that even your confusion was something you could feel guilty about. Everyone in the room seemed to understand with perfect clarity what was going on, except you. Unless it was the other way around, and it was just you who understood, the acrylic sweater almost in your hands.

In any case the moment was a thing you turned over again and again—the purple and blue argyles, the flash of gold liquid, the cracked glaze of your mother's cosmetic face, the slick way the acrylic is about to feel in your hands, and which has to do, you know, with the size of your father's paycheck—turned again and again like a paperweight in which snow falls in stiff white flakes like tinsel, falls as it turns in your mind's eye, falls through some synthetic viscous fluid that is nothing like air, nothing like anything breathable, nothing like what it pretends to be. At last you realize this is a possession of yours, and that, in a way, you never wanted to resolve it because then it would dissolve, it would be lost to you, and the thing is, after all, a lovesake.

A moment of time can be a thing. It can be an object in which meaning coheres, glitters, pours, establishes a new meniscus. Between various particular moments a surface tension can form that is so forceful you can set needles and razor blades on it, and they will float as if transcendent. They are not transcendent. They must be able to prick and slash. Before a thing can be a symbol it must be a thing. It must do its job as a thing in the world before and during and after you have projected all your meaning all over it.

What is most sublime is not far from the body. Rembrandt's portraits, so psychological, merely depict light and darkness falling on the surfaces of faces. Notes of music are often just strings of different lengths set vibrating, which sets a thing vibrating inside your ear. Taste—Lord knows what taste is, but it is due to the nose and the tongue. My father ate tongue, and it used to shock me, the big pink cow's tongue the size of a hand, plump, pliant, coated with desiccated, dimpling white taste buds, an actual tongue that looked exactly like a giant human tongue flopped on the white plastic of the fridge door in see-through Saran near the eggs. How would that tongue taste on his tongue? How did he have the nerve? I wondered the same thing when he ordered brains once in a restaurant as if it was the most ordinary thing. He had not said, "You know what? I think I'm going to order brains. What the hell! You only live once! You've got to try everything." No, he perused the menu, shut it, listened to the family's dinner conversation, perhaps added a comment or two, and, when the waiter inclined his head toward him, he said "Brains," not loudly and not softly, just matter-of-factly, and, being a somewhat subdued person much of the time, he ate the brains the same way.

He found them somewhat disappointing. "They were a little . . . loose," he said, when asked. He didn't think he'd order them again. Still, he didn't leave them over, and he didn't choke them down while making a face. He ate the brains, which I recall looked like lumpy brownish scrambled eggs, without much commentary, with a sort of matter-of-fact aplomb. There were things in the world. He meant to know them. This is the same modest fearlessness with which he keeps a stickball bat propped near the broom closet in case he needs to clobber a mouse, the same modest fearlessness with which he seizes the plunger and advances on a clogged toilet, no matter how bad—it comes of sitting up with sick children, I think, and coming running in the night when someone screams (it turned out not to be a burglar, but clothes), and patiently dripping eyedrops in a child's glued-shut eyes, or offering his own Neo-Synephrine, which he assures will "clear you right up!" It is a complete disregard for squeamishness when faced with the things of this world that amounts to a sort of bravery. He can quote Goethe and knows most of the operas performed at the Met, but the things of the world aren't below him.

I used to think what was meaningful was incorporeal. But how can we point to the moon without a finger? And the moon! Even that floating symbol has a mass of 810 trillion tons, and heaves the oceans toward it, and grabs at even the blood in women's bodies. Nothing is that pure. My husband saw a Chasid at a girlie show once. I saw a Buddhist in a train compartment muttering his soft chant over and over, rocking in place, as if to make my girlfriends and me, or he himself, vanish from the train. All the while he gazed out the dark window, though, one of my friends said later, she saw he was actually staring at us mirrored back. We are all bodies in the world, and our stories are the stories of bodies. To write meaningfully, we must grasp that. And that is all we must grasp.

This is marvelous news! We do not need a big idea to write! We do not need to know why or even if our story is important!

We do not need to have something to say! "Art is being rid of all preaching," Virginia Woolf says. "Things in themselves; the sentence in itself is beautiful: multitudinous, seas; daffodils that come before the swallow dares." And Cezanne: "The day is coming when a single carrot, freshly observed, will set off a revolution."

We can do this: we can observe. We can take our pens and write what we see, what we hear. Who sits in the coffee shop smoking cigarette after cigarette? How does she hold her head, and with exactly what expression does she inhale? Does she add too much milk to her coffee, so that it sloshes toward the top, and then does she hardly sip it at all? Does she gulp it swiftly, black? Something is on this person's mind. We might conjecture, but first the reader must see her, must hear what she says. People are incessantly expressive. We sing ourselves every instant, with our bitten lips, our constrained voices, our message machines, our walk, our run, our way of stepping onto a bus, our compulsion to apologize, our lust to accuse, our styles of hugging and kissing.

Once in my life I kissed a woman on the mouth romantically. The surprising thing about it was that she kissed in the exact same way she held a pencil and walked down the street in sandals and shook salt into a bowl of soup. Her gestures had a coherence that was utterly natural. I had expected a secret to be revealed when I kissed her, but discovered that she expressed her secret constantly, as we all do, night and day.

A writer's work, then, is to let us see what is being said. Daily life is always extraordinary when rendered precisely. We can unlock our lives with a pencil tip.

This is why people read: to have experiences. We have all had experiences. We have them every day. We had profound ones being our parents' children, falling in love, falling out of love, traveling somewhere or other, traveling back. If they are profound to us, we can make them profound to a reader, but it takes work: we must let the reader see what we saw, touch what we touched, hear what we thought and felt. To see an ordinary thing clearly is highly unusual. Most people live beneath ceilings they have never looked at, shop in supermarkets they have never seen, feel they hardly know what—they lack the tool of a notebook and a pen, the tool of sentences that drive one forward with their pressing logic. The very structure of a sentence is logical; to complete a sentence one must complete the thought.

Leonardo da Vinci walked around with a small sketchpad strapped to his belt. He drew people walking; running; being angry, pensive, happy, sad. He did not think he was through with seeing. He observed incessantly. How happy this makes me! How full of life and action I see the world suddenly is! As I write it down I see that even the most rote thing, the way my husband and I part for work in the morning, say, is in fact always new.

Paul's blue pinstripe suit has frayed at the belt loops; white lines like tiny vertical grins have appeared. He refuses to buy another suit because a suit is not supposed to wear out in two years. This morning he sat on the porch at the rickety wood coffee table with the wasp's nest growing underneath. The back door open, he listened to his Italian records, something he never did in the morning before. A man with a smooth, deep voice enunciates clearly, rolling his *r*'s.

"Portogallo," the man says, modeling suave assurance.

"Portogallo," Paul replies.

"Egitto," proclaims the man.

Paul answers, "Egitto," nodding his head.

He fetched the little records from the library last week. They were issued in 1956 and boast a method perfected by the U.S. Department of War.

"*Buon giorno!*" Paul called as he left.

We were both nervous. He has a new boss; I had a girlfriend angry at me, or, rather, I was angry at her. This too was something new. People have been angry at me for years; after many months of psychotherapy, though, I was at last angry at someone else and *knew* it. I was rather proud of myself. It recalled to me a strange proverb my mother recently told me her own mother said. "Better that she should be angry than that you should be angry," my hard-working, widowed grandmother said. How it made me wish I were she! The anger of others paralyzed me. Apologies flew from my lips. This new thing, though, my own anger, seemed like a marvelous achievement, like learning to drive.

"*Buon giorno!*" I said, strolling down the blacktop and waving.

"*Arrivederci!*" Paul called—and I realized how much of this new language I already knew.

All this could become part of a short story. Stories hang from the trees, hive under the coffee table, gather like glass on the corners of the roads. To pick them up one needs simply to focus one's eye and keep a steady hand. Writing focuses the eye; writing develops the steadiness of one's hand. And what the stories mean becomes unavoidable; the meaning is the part that takes care of itself. Render the world precisely on paper, and you will see the stories it holds. There they are, warm, buzzing, continually close, prepared to remain invisible forever if one chooses to overlook them, prepared to reveal all their secrets to the observant eye, the hand that continues despite the risks.

The body pulls the soul after it. Your eye knows more than you think. Telling how to draw a person, Stan Lee of Marvel Comics says, "Heads are generally five eyes wide." Let us see each of those five eyes with each of our five eyes. Your eyes never existed before on this earth. Let us see what they see, and you will have told us as powerfully as possible more than you know.

ANOREXIA OF LANGUAGE: WHY WE CAN'T WRITE

I HAVE BEEN STARING INTO SILENCE'S blank face all month, and I want to rattle it, to shake it, to force it to confess what's at its obsessive, fanatic core.

This is our first real encounter. Before this, I'd hardly met with silence at all. When I came across others who suffered with it, who could not write and yearned to, I was mystified. What was the big deal? It was like watching someone writhe in an invisible straitjacket. What are you doing? you ask. Don't you know you are free? I'd written for so many years without being blocked that I thought I was immune. And I was full of advice, the advice of one who has an answer while scarcely understanding the question.

Now I am amazed at the power of silence's chill presence. The air is so brittle it feels it will crack. How hard it is to breathe! I feel so unwell, so bizarrely estranged from myself. Some key part of me has been kidnapped, stolen, swallowed by silence. "Spit it out!" I want to cry, but I know it won't spit.

If silence is anything, it's decorous. Its face opposite me is flawlessly made up. Its hands are folded neatly on its knees, and it is good as any schoolchild, slim to the point of vanishing, with not a hair out of place as it gazes at me with lucid blue eyes. It is stronger than I, I fear. I feel like a bad psychiatrist, judgmental and punishing. I have an urge to slam the desk and shout, "Why are you doing this to me? You're ruining my career! Be good! Speak, goddamn it!"

Silence swallows. She stares at me in pain as if to say she cannot help herself. If she could—oh, the volumes she'd say! There'd be no stopping her. But—

"But what? Say it! *But. What?*"

Her eyes break from mine and roam the room as if searching for a correlative to point to, something that will illustrate what she means. She finds nothing, and shrugs. Her restraint is perfect, virginal, absolute. In all this time she has said nothing for which she could be blamed. Yet her eyes shine with desire! "If only, if only—" her whole body seems to say, her hands twisted, her legs crossed.

Her presence makes me frantic. Alone with silence, I want to eat, dash from the house, wash the dishes, sleep. Panic fills me. I feel sick. I feel I will dissolve in the face of silence, and then it will have triumphed. I will be infected by it and grow mute. What would I be? A petrified woman, calcified, stone-hard. Knock on it—no resonance. Touch it—it is cold as granite, drawing heat from your hand.

Here is the fear silence breeds: you will be a person shut up inside yourself, shut up like an old apartment building with windows of brick and doors of cinderblock.

Since I have sat with silence, friends have entrusted stories to me. The same thing sometimes happens to pregnant women or people who have been in accidents—horror stories arrive. Even relative strangers stop to impart the tale of a particularly gruesome delivery or of a paralyzing whiplash that manifested all of a sudden a full month later, when the person in the car crash thought everything was okay ("One moment he was sitting there eating his coleslaw, the next—*bam!*—his neck had turned to iron!").

"I knew a woman who won a Radcliffe Bunting Fellowship,"

my friend Stacia says. "Suddenly she couldn't write. Every day she went to the office they provided and just sat there. Five months went by like this, and then she could write again."

Five months! What a torture!

"What changed for her?"

Over the phone, I practically hear Stacia shrug. "I don't know, actually. I don't think she ever said."

My friend Joel says, "It can take years to get over a block. It's been three years since I signed my book contract, and I haven't written a chapter since then."

Joel, my dear friend Joel! It never occurred to me that he might be blocked about his book. I thought he merely chose to write other things or not to write at all, he seems to live with such easy grace. But my silence has let him tell about his.

"Years?" I say.

"Yes, years to forget there is an editor waiting for your work, years until you are sure the editor has forgotten your name."

Ah: one must be sure one's editor has forgotten one's name.

In Joel's desk lies an embossed document bearing the imprint of a distant company and below it Joel's name signed in his own hand promising to deliver his entire book by a certain specific date. Now Joel can visualize an editor outside himself, an editor with a face that is not Joel's own. He hardly knows this man. He has met him once or twice. How can he be sure to please him? Joel is free to project onto this man all the astringent disapproval he himself often feels about his own work. Now he has a contract and editor outside himself to reinforce the ones within.

I call my friend Alice, who dropped out of graduate school with seven incompletes because she couldn't do her papers. Certainly she triumphed over her block—she works for a computer company now, writing software manuals. What's her solution?

"Computer stuff is a game," she says. "It doesn't really matter to me. I write about what I do not passionately care about. You'll notice I don't write about art history," she says, which was her field of study.

And now it occurs to me that I myself worked for a professor who was blocked. I just didn't recognize it. He had been awarded permission to write the official biography of a certain towering literary critic, a man this professor had devoted his entire life to studying. How many years have elapsed since then! And still his book has not appeared (oh, "appeared"!—as if we wrote in closets, as if our writing was a personal delusion until it erupted, Athena-like, sporelike, into bookstores!). This professor labored over his paragraphs, stuffing them fuller and fuller of gratuitous erudition, references for their own sake (or, rather, for *his* own sake), refusing to let them split into other paragraphs—perhaps because his subject, the eminent literary critic, had a quirk of long paragraphs—until each paragraph was at least two pages and so crammed it was virtually unreadable. Flow? The poor man himself could hardly breathe under the pressure of it all!

At the time he seemed silly to me, a buffoonish creature, red-faced, sweat flying off him, gasping from his run up my stairs at one o'clock, starved, scavenging for a slice of bread I begrudged him, ripping open a packet of Vitamin C powder ("Bursting with the power of Citrus!" it said in neon orange on a blue field) from a box he left in my kitchen like a claim on me—a lover's memento, and I resented that too—desperate to show me the paragraphs he'd corrected and recorrected, adding and erasing, and adding, always adding more with his exquisitely sharpened pencils (those flanks of pencils!) with their neatly beveled pink rubber caps, adding until his paragraphs seized up like an engine without oil, impenetrable.

"What do you think?" he asked.

"Um, it's fine. It's just terrific. I think you can move on now."

"You really think so? You think it's terrific?"

"Yes, I do. Although, you know"—what imp prodded me?— "I think you might be able to cut a bit. But you can do that later, when you're all done, when it's time to edit."

"Cut? Where?" And he seized the sheet and stared at it, but instead of cutting he added even more.

I regarded him from my station behind the hulking gray IBM typewriter he had brought me. It was as heavy as a stove, consumed more than half my kitchen table, and seemed capable of typing *Ulysses* a couple of dozen times before it would need servicing. I sighed and glowered and tapped my foot, and did not offer him cheese or butter to go with the bread he wolfed from my fridge.

And yet he returned. I was hired merely to type his manuscript, but had myself become magically endowed with the power to help, to *help*—until at last he traveled a thousand miles, lugging valises full of reference books, and going to the expense of a hotel so I could type for him and talk a bit. At the time it seemed merely strange and comic (it was too odd to be flattering), although I was grateful for the money and the interesting work—but now it seems poignant.

Here was a man struggling for his life. How could he construct a book so firm and big and steady he could pile his whole life on top and not sink? How could he write a book so masculine and intelligent, so extraordinarily intelligent, it would be worthy of his terrifying, Freudian-freighted, large-craniumed subject? This man, this professor, did not even have his own name! Or, rather, the name he had was the same name his father and grandfather had had and that his son now bore, too. Each of them, to commemorate the fact of their separate identity, had been given a Roman numeral—an I—to accrue to the family moniker, and they had all graduated from the same Ivy League school ("My father's father, my father, and I all attended Yale," he announced, as if they went as a group. To his discomfort, his son was toying with the idea of Swarthmore), and it was as if now this man must salvage them all, must show he deserves to be one, must, must—what? Do something that will endure the scrutiny of that gathering of namesakes, an ancestral corridor of portraits all bearing his own face. Struggling for his life? Oh, yes. Struggling at the age of about fifty to prove that his own separate I has not been in vain.

The trick, obviously, to writing such a book is to give up on oneself. It is to evade oneself, to push one's own resistant ego down into the hot close darkness and hope to get some work done before the thing springs out of its jack-in-the-box again. It is to take a leap of faith.

When Kierkegaard writes about the leap of faith, he means an act that makes no sense, a bargain that is no bargain—one makes the ultimate sacrifice, gives up that which is at one's core, that which one understood perhaps to be the very purpose of one's life—and at that very instant of relinquishment, "by virtue of the absurd," one gets it back, redeemed. But the key point is, you don't know you will get it back. When you make the sacrifice, you *really* make it.

Kierkegaard takes as his text Abraham and Isaac. God asked for the sacrifice of Isaac, specifying to Abraham that He wanted "your son, your favored one, Isaac, whom you love." Why put it like this? It is as if God wanted Abraham to know He was acutely aware of just what He was asking. And the very next sentence of the story says Abraham saddled his ass and split the wood. When the time came he bound Isaac, laid him on the altar, and "picked up his knife to slay his son." He was going to do it. He was doing it. He did not hold back. His faith was so true—the way a bird's flight is said to be true—that he would sacrifice, bloodily, with his own sweating hands, the child he loved.

A dazzling story. And, like the story of Job, it is so dangerous it is preceded by the reassurance that this devout man is just being put "to the test," so that the reader is spared from being in Abraham's or Job's position even in imagination. Who but they wouldn't lose faith when confronted with this infinite demand? Kierkegaard tells the story over and over in *Fear and Trembling* as if he could not pull his mind from it, as if, always, the story itself had even more latent power.

For, according to Kierkegaard, the contradiction is that Abraham felt that God was asking him to murder his son *and* that He was good. That was the leap of faith. Not bitterly, not renouncing the joys of this earth like some sort of abstracted glaze-eyed monk, but with his eyes clear and love in his veins, Abraham lifted the knife. He gave up his reason. He leapt. "To be able to lose one's reason, and therefore the whole of finiteness of which reason is the broker," Kierkegaard writes, "and then by virtue of the absurd to gain precisely the same finiteness—that appalls my soul, but I do not for this cause say that it is something lowly, since on the contrary it is the only prodigy . . . The dialectic of faith is the finest and most remarkable of all."

To gain the book, one must give up all hope for the book. It is the only way the book can get written. While one writes one cannot simultaneously be gazing up at a glorious, abstract painting of what the book should be, a painting that is all golden glow and admirable wordless heft conveying a sense of a book like a bible, like your very own bible, penned by you—and at the same time expect to be advancing into the body of this particular earthly book. It won't work. You may gaze and gaze, but you may be sure that when you begin to write, that gorgeous ineffable volume will not coalesce on the page. Something else will appear. And then you have a choice. You can accept it, and get on with your writing, or you can throw it away, and pine for the painting. It is so beautiful! When you're not actually writing, you have the feeling it would be so simple to get it down on paper. Yet when the time comes, your sentences tangle you. They knot and seethe, grasping like desperate children, hampering you and making you fall so that the beautiful book, the infinite book, is forever out of reach.

The only way is to set the unbook—the gilt-framed painting of the book—right there on the altar and sacrifice it, truly sacrifice it. Only then may the book, the real live flawed finite book, slowly, sentence by carnal sentence, appear. Leopold Bloom starts his day by eating a slightly burnt grilled kidney which imparts "to his palate a fine tang of faintly scented urine." Even from here literature may begin.

*   *   *

All of which is easily said.

The *Tao Te Ching* says, "Care about people's approval / and you will be their prisoner." I nod my head and copy it into my notebook. This does not free me from caring about people's approval.

Well, I can read the words over and over. I can plaster them to every square inch of my room. I can quote them and expound on them and tattoo them onto my flesh. It would be like a fetish, though: I almost expect the words to perform the transformation for me. It is as though I hope to hypnotize myself with them. It is as though I want to mesmerize myself with them through a ritual rhythm the way the Bushmen were said to mesmerize themselves, to enchant themselves, to induce a trance state for themselves so that a vision could come, an ecstatic experience beyond what they could reach with their ordinary minds. How does one change?

The Bushmen had visions of being what they hunted, what gave them life: an eland. They had visions of being dead, of being under water—a fish—and they returned from the trance swimming back toward life, their arms gliding, swimming back into the rhythmic pounding of stamping feet. People in the community had to touch them, had to welcome their bodies with their own patting hands so that they could fully return, so that they could be here now.

This was where wisdom came from: surrendering to what is beyond yourself, where your self is not. Discovering that you are part of an existence that is greater than you, that is greater than even your humanity, although you may experience this only when your thinking self is quenched. How not to eat humbly, to walk lightly, with gratitude, afterward? On the mountain where Abraham lifted the knife to slay Isaac, he also had a vision. "And Abraham named that site Adonai-yireh," the Bible says, "whence the present saying, 'On the mount of the LORD there is vision.'" What vision? That relinquishment will bring plenty; that faith returns what you love to you, dazzling, redeemed.

Most of us must go on without a vision, though. We are bereft of the experience that ravishes and transforms. We cling to what is dear to us; we safeguard it under lock and key. We are leery of the surrender that it takes to write. We want to have our vision before we begin, before we lift the knife to slay what we love, our cherished egos, our desire to be excellent. We want them back before we give them up. Not later, but now we want our vision. Not as reward but as guarantee.

If only the knowledge that one must have faith provided faith! If only advice transformed us, instead of remaining something external if correct, something easy to agree with but remote as someone talking on TV.

So far I have tried to say everything in this essay well. I have tried to say it beautifully, and that is a sort of strain. What I've really meant to say, what I really care about saying, I have not said. If I say enough beautiful things, I feel, I will earn the right to say what I really mean. Then I can take that risk.

It is possible to write whole novels this way. I have written a few this way myself, the whole thing one gigantic preamble to what I really mean to write about. One novel about a ménage à trois starts a full year earlier, in a different country altogether, where the two women in the triangle meet. Oh, the pleasure of writing about fields of withering sunflowers and women in black trudging up rocky streets, and shops the size of closets devoted solely to three- and five-cent rolls, and gaunt, writhing images of Jesus with eyes like steel darts—hundreds of pages can be spent on this, while in the back of her mind the writer cries, "Wait! Wait! The good part is about to come! Just a few more chapters!" so that when the reader at last arrives at the ménage, it is with predictable fatigue, and the writer rushes the crucial scenes. It is like a person who waits until the whole room is nodding on the verge of sleep before producing from her purse the pages she waited all evening to share, or like a student giving an oral report and dutifully enumerating the mineral and agricultural endowments of the assigned country while her face pounds with the marvelous anecdote she can hardly wait to tell, the shocking anecdote that brought the whole country alive to her (she wants to say, "Chile is shaped like a woman's leg! It's like the leg of a woman in a chorus line, which reminds me of something that happened in Santiago once . . . ") but which she suppresses, hoping there's time for it in the end. If there's time, it will probably be the one thing the class remembers about Chile. If there's not time, she will have delivered an organized, thorough report of no real importance to her or probably anyone else. And yet, even as an adult, how hard it is to trust that what you care about really matters! How much easier it is to spend one's time doing what the schoolteacher inside oneself would think is good. One hoards what matters, unwilling to risk ridicule. One tries to say things beautifully—I try to say things beautifully—and puts off saying what one really means.

I am not sure that what I really mean to say is beautiful or extraordinary. I identify with it, and not with the more formal things I've already said. The somewhat "strained" things I've written (I think of a strainer holding back the irregular, hard-to-digest clumps and seeds and allowing the smooth sauce of style to slide through) serve the purpose of telling me that I can write decently: they remind me of things I've written that people liked. And I need that.

Every day I must prove to myself I am a writer. The knowledge goes away in my sleep. What I wrote yesterday was paltry, meager, so flawed it is barely anything. Or, if it is good, I am no longer the person who could write it. In either case—shame or approval—it is utterly separate from me, that piece of writing, as if a skin formed on it like the skin on pudding when it chills, a thin, rubbery, albumenlike skin separating it from me. I am insufficient again.

And every day I must reach down into myself and see if the place that makes writing exists. Is it still there? The only way to know is to write, but before I write, and while I am at the beginning of writing, and before I hear the voice of the piece, before it speaks through me, there is this anxiety, this panic, this lack of belief. I don't feel it! It's gone! In my sleep an operation must have happened, an amputation, and now I am hollow. Or I've been anaesthetized, and now the part of me that writes is asleep, a sort of exquisite, morbid Snow White sleep, the waking voice irrecoverable for 100 years.

Why should this be? Why this perpetual sense of doubt and loss?

A friend of mine who has a young daughter wakes up at four-thirty in the morning to write. She says she does it not so much for the writing, but because if she doesn't do it she feels like an aspirin tablet in water: dissolving. "I am that tablet," she says, and I hear in that the strength of her being a writing tablet and the terror that she will dissolve and disappear.

Is this terror more common to some of us? Are some of us prone to dissolving, like the witch in *The Wizard of Oz?* (How sorry I felt for her just at that moment when she cried in anguish, "I'm mellllllting!" As much as I'd hated her before, suddenly I was overwhelmed by such remorse, such shocking guilt and sympathy! She was my own mother, then! At the last instant I recognized her!) Some of us seem actually *designed* to give way. Women especially are raised to be so extremely sensitive to others we feel permeable; we are so accustomed to swallowing our wants before they even reach consciousness that a bewildering, uneasy passivity often persists in us. At worst, we even resent our own feelings. We experience them as intrusive. It is as if the emotional part of ourselves is a stubborn, fleshy, disruptive, and even aggressive appendage (aggressive because it causes such wrenching disharmonies between ourselves and those we love), and we resent it so intensely that we half wish to amputate it, to carve it out of ourselves and toss it in the garbage, this lump of self like an inflamed tonsil or hermaphroditic, mistaken penis—half wish to amputate it even though it is the very thing that keeps us *from* dissolving—and half wish to annihilate the Other, the beloved, who has made such an enemy out of what we know to be most absolutely essential to our self, and without which no true pleasure, no true anything, is possible.

The fear of anaesthesia is related to the wish for anaesthesia. The terror of a midnight amputation is connected to a devout wish for just such an event, as well as to the actual sense-memory of amputations, experiences of dissociating from a part of oneself because it is too frighteningly disruptive.

But where do we imagine real writing comes from? Can we suppose that we may be missing a vital organ or two and yet write? Or that we may be internally bound and gagged, and yet still wield a pen? So many of us would prefer to dissolve ourselves and reconvene elsewhere. So many of us, practiced in administering our own internal morphine, wish to preserve harmony at all cost, to be good wives and virtuous daughters, yet write. We disregard the fugitive emotion we are not supposed to feel, and whose presence we do not understand.

I phoned a friend to tell her something I had said only once or twice before in my life. My throat clenched, my heart banging, I said that I was hurt and even angry about something she'd done. Within five minutes I was holding the phone to my ear, listening to her sob. The reason she'd hurt me, she explained, had to do with her own suffering, of which my complaint reminded her. Through her tears she told me how hard things were for her these days. Yet how familiar they were, her tears! I felt quite distant suddenly, as if something in me had been short-circuited, or as if I'd forgotten something important, pressing her sobs to my ear sitting on the hard, grimy kitchen floor.

I tried to accept her tears as a gift, as intimate self-revelation, as the nonaggressive reason for her earlier hurtful behavior. Why did part of me feel left out? Her tears again! How often I had sat with the phone crammed against my ear, held hostage by her tears. I felt far away, and even bored while she wept, as if this were something I had no choice but to wait out if I was going to be a decent human being—and at the same time I felt monstrous for my cold reaction to her tears. What was wrong with me? Of course I didn't mention my feeling. It was nonsensical to me, and I tried not to see it. After we said good-bye, I drifted away from the phone, drifted into the living room, a benign emotion surrounding me like fog.

"How was your phone call?" my husband asked.

"Oh, fine, fine." I blinked, and sighed.

Only the next day, when a friend suggested a new analysis, did I understand what the nonsensical emotion meant. I would rather not have known. I would have preferred to go on feeling that vague, drifty, blissful intimacy with my friend rather than the renewed blaze of anger. I had been, I felt, at peace.

How tempting it is to choose this apparent peace! And because so many of us are trained to do so, how evanescent is our sense of self.

Time and again my students tell me, "I am here to find my voice." I want to say, "When did you lose it, and how? Where did you hear it last? Try to remember every place you have been since then and maybe it will occur to you where you lost it." Some of us are like deaf people who need someone to place our hands on our throats. Feel this? This is you, speaking. Some of us need it pointed out: this is your arm, this is your leg, this is your voice. Yes, here. Right here. Can you hear it? It sounds like you.

And some of us, even able to hear our own voice, are overwhelmed by a sense of its unimportance.

"I am paralyzed by the conviction that no one would be interested in what I have to say, or how I say it," wrote a friend in a letter a few years ago.

"I no longer feel special enough to write anything but facile responses to assigned exercises," another woman, a student of mine, said.

A third reported, "I feel petrified by the pressure." In a ten-minute freewrite, this student produced just one sentence. It was the only writing she offered all semester long, although she routinely provided lacerating critiques of the novels we read.

The feeling of nullity, the suspicion of internal anaesthesia—these were not strangers to me. They were familiar phantoms I'd lived in the company of my whole life without ever really noticing. I did not notice because as long as I could work, my life was by definition okay. Only when these emotions became a paralyzing constant and the writing would not come—only then did I fully perceive these feelings and question them.

My silence was an anorexic, I began to see. Over the weeks we were together, this trait became more and more apparent. She refused to open her mouth for any purpose. She presided over herself with an iron tyranny. Her bones sought the surface as if she were proud of them. Her blue eyes, burning fiercely, sank into her skull, and her legs grew spindly, yellowish, like stilts, as if—if she rose—she would be balanced above her body, as if only her face was really her self. Her face loomed now above her dwindling body as if trying to break free.

And then, late one tense but tedious afternoon, an afternoon when we had sat across from each other so long, so rigidly, it seemed we would always be locked like this, I realized that perhaps she *was* trying to communicate. She seemed to be X-raying herself. She seemed to be burning the opaque flesh from herself. She seemed to be unwrapping herself, paring the bark off herself, pressing some horrible, intolerable thought out of the core of herself. Her whole body was an Adam's apple about to spring through the skin. Why, that was it! That's all it was! She was showing the structure of herself, exposing the very composition of herself, making visible to the world the most basic anatomical unit of a self that would not be compromised, that possessed an inherent unbudging rigidity.

Look, each rib and joint seemed to say, I am real. I exist. Unlikely as it seems in this girl who has been so compliant for so very long—momma's angel, daddy's special darling (you could see it in the Peter Pan collar, the dainty pearl earrings, the hands so scrubbed they looked chapped, the nails bitten to the point of extinction)—there is a hard spine, a pith of rock, a blazing brick-hard calcareous stick.

"Perfectionistic behavior elicits approval from parents and teachers, who think of the potentially anorexic child as unusually good and competent," reports Hilda Bruch. I read her work with rapt attention. Because even without personifying silence, it would still be clear that writer's block is a form of anorexia. Reading Bruch, I was astonished at how much I saw myself in her description of the anorexic's childhood, and how thoroughly it related to my battle with silence. "Some of the more serious conceptual disturbances can be traced to this pseudosuccess of being praised and recognized for fake good behavior," she says. "This praise reinforces the anorexic's fear of being spontaneous and natural, and interferes with her developing concepts, especially a vocabulary for her true feelings, or even her ability to identify feelings . . .

"Future anorexics are described as serious, precocious in their sense of responsibility, trustworthy, and capable of having adult conversations . . . When maintaining this facade becomes too strenuous, they finally protest and express their underlying frustration by giving up the behavior that they themselves call 'fake.'

"Superficially the relationship to the parents appears to be congenial: actually it is too close, with too much involvement, without necessary separation and individuation. This harmony . . . is achieved through excessive conformity on the part of the child. After the illness has existed for some time, glaring hostility becomes evident."

Here is the rebellion of pent-up girlhood. Here is the onslaught of the virtuous. Here is the revolt of the good by means of excessive goodness. Here is the break with the mother by means of breaking with oneself, denying one's own needs more and more ruthlessly. One girl, Bruch reports, saw her shadow on the beach and vowed to get as thin as it. Perfection is being a gaunt substanceless figure projected on the earth. It must be what the mother unwittingly taught: that this girl should be a specter riveted to her creator, inseparable from her, echoing and mirroring and forever called to heel, racing over the sands to keep pace, able to tolerate her own self only if it displayed the utmost pleasant obedience.

The rebellion, when it comes, baffles the rebel. Her reasons, her own history in fact, are cloudy to her. Bruch reports: "It is quite difficult for most anorexics to present the facts as they have taken place, because their upbringing did not foster clear and independent observation and thinking."

Happiness for this child is pleasing the mother, bringing home an A, several A's, on which to feed her. It is walking, mother and daughter, with arms wrapped around each other, a few feet ahead of everyone else at the girl's camp open house. The girl, myself, is fifteen already, wearing a beige Huckapoo blouse that snaps at the crotch, blue jeans, and long brown hair flooding from a central part, leaving visible just a narrow plank of her face like someone peering through a scarcely open door. Her hips bump her mother's awkwardly, embarrassingly from time to time. What a superlative relationship I have with my mother, she thinks proudly, noticing another girl who maintains from that girl's mother a surly distance of at least two feet. How can she? Isn't the mother hurt? What a horrible, brutish, sloppy daughter that is!—like her very own sister, in fact, who in a rage heaves the bedroom door shut so it booms like a cannon and plaster clatters down. The plaster seems to fall within their own fragile mother.

This daughter, the pleasant one, never plays rock music at home: she doesn't own a record although there is a record player in the living room and dozens of classical recordings. The loud noise would bother her mother, or else her mother would sit tensely waiting it out: what was the pleasure there? Once when she was thirteen a girlfriend had given her the album to *Hair* with its greenish yellow psychedelic boy on the cover. At the girlfriend's house she'd love to lie down right beside the speaker turned on high: it was thrilling! A teenage virgin, LBJ, dropping out, Timothy Leary—and the syncopation made her smile. But when her friend gave her a copy for her birthday—what a great friend she was! how she loved her for this—she had given it back after a few days. She couldn't imagine playing it in her parents' apartment. She couldn't bear even to have it in the apartment, couldn't bear to have her parents' eyes even see it.

She doesn't drink Pepsi, this daughter, only Coke. In fact, she is angry at Pepsi. What's wrong with the drink of the older generation? Why does the new generation need its own drink? The commercials actually hurt her, fill her with a painful wistfulness like seeing gray in her father's hair. Most special are the evenings at Daffodil Hill in the Botanical Gardens, listening to opera, her contented parents gazing at the lit-up orchestra. The only bad part is the walk back to the car through the park, stumbling in the night with just her father's wobbly small yellow flashlight beam to find their way, the dark figures of other people brushing past them, vaguely hostile, so uncaring of her parents' uneasy progress. What a relief when they find their own car! They lock the doors, keeping the rushing unstoppable distended aggressive figures out. Inside the small space of the car all is peaceful. Threats come only from outside.

Which is to say that although the eventual anorexia is a rebellion, it is impossible for the daughter to know this. She is doing what she had been taught to do, with a vengeance.

The poet Louise Glück writes, "In mid-adolescence, I developed a symptom perfectly congenial to the demands of my spirit. I had great resources of will and no self . . . I couldn't say what I was, what I wanted, in any day-to-day, practical way. What I could say was no: the way I saw to separate myself, to establish a self with clear boundaries, was to oppose myself to the declared desire of others, utilizing their wills to give a shape to my own . . . The tragedy of anorexia seems to me that its intent is not self-destructive, though its outcome so often is. Its intent is to construct, in the only way possible when means are so limited, a plausible self."

The conviction of internal emptiness, the fear of being spontaneous, the rigid barrier between oneself and one's emotions—all this pertains to silence, which orders one to prove one's worth day by day.

I became unable to write at the moment of my success. On the basis of a proposal, I had at last sold a book. When I sat down to write it, though, I found myself paralyzed.

It was not that I could not think. I could think. It was not that I'd forgotten what I wanted to say. I knew exactly what I wanted to say. I merely could not grab hold of the words and stick them to the page. They seemed to float away from me into shadowy depths. It was exactly the same sensation as being unable to remember a word: you can heft the precise length of the word in your mind, you know that it starts with a *b* perhaps or a *p*, and maybe even where on a certain page of *Love in the Time of Cholera* you read this word—but the word itself won't come. It resists you. It is like a cloaked figure you encounter, whose body you *know*—why, the instant you see who it is you will cry, "Of course! I knew it all along!"—but who won't throw off his hood. How tantalizing, this information held just out of reach! Not being able to think of a word duplicates writer's block exactly, except that writer's block is more protracted, and envelops one's whole vocabulary.

Being unable to write also felt like having the key to me stolen. I had not even known there was a key to me, and now I found it gone! It was as if I had been secured in a sort of invisible chastity belt, my most intimate parts locked behind an iron gate (again, I did not imagine these parts were not there; I simply no longer had access to them), my master having vanished with the key. It was an eerie and frightening experience. I believed I was self-possessed. One day the key was turned, and I found I'd been living my life in a see-through cage.

I sat bolt upright at the desk in a sort of rigid agony, unable to do more than put one or two meager words on the page which I instantly discarded before casting about for more slow minutes for some more words. My mind swam in a haze while my body was stiff, contracted, as if all the space between my bones had vanished, and they were stuck against one another. At last I stood, yawned, and burst into tears.

I was not surprised. I had entered a time when I cried every day at some time or another. I had never in my life been a crier; now my heart was a great big bloated painful thing like an infected foot, and the least pressure on it made it burst. I learned to drive crying, and pee crying, and even read a book crying, stopping only occasionally to wipe my eyes so the words didn't meld. Often I didn't wipe my eyes, though. I liked the feeling of my face slick with tears—it stung, and felt shiny—because at least these tears were something real, something that came spontaneously from within me at a time when nothing else would. They meant that something was going on even if I didn't know what.

I imagined that the missing key to me was something very ordinary. It was, I supposed, something small and cheap as the key to a diary, inconsequential as a flip-top. It was dull silver as the key to a tin of sardines whose lid curls stiffly back to reveal multiple flattened twin-eyed faces numberless as a pack of sperm, each one shaped like a slimy key.

A thousand keys, a million keys, the key of C, of A and B, the key to the city, to the riddle, to the silver skates, and to the whole cascade of typewriter keys, those keys like *Ziegfeld Follies*, in tiers, or like the Palisades, a glacial ebb: QAZ, WSX. There was a whole kingdom of keys locked away from me. It was multitudinous as the bevy of keys in my mother's drawer, keys to places where we had not lived for decades, to forgotten neighbors' apartments and lost jewelry boxes, to underground storage rooms holding childhood Flexible Flyers and one-speed bikes, keys with dust clinging to them and smelling so strongly of steel your mouth filled with the taste, keys with ragged teeth that looked random and nonsensical now that the doors for them were gone. All lost to me. To be able to write is to unlock imaginary rooms that contain real keys, to adapt Marianne Moore's statement. My master key was gone. It was an object so obvious that it was invisible, like something you lose in your own house, and which only someone else can find.

Who had found my key?

The publisher, I assumed. My writing had always been the one thing that was all my own. I'd sold it, and now it avoided me.

I phoned the editor and told her not to expect the manuscript for a long, long time.

But I still felt spooked. One day someone was standing in the room with me. My back and neck prickled. I spun my head and stared at the empty gray space behind me, the mound of laundry near the door. I had the urge, like a child, to glance in the closets. Someone was stealing from me, someone was watching me, someone was doing a terrible thing to me. I had no defense against it.

This was the worst. It was even worse than not writing: the feeling of being absolutely porous, without barriers, as if anyone at any time of day or night could open the door and walk in, as if the key to me had been duplicated a million times and strewn all over the world, and now anyone could come and take.

I had begun to write a little bit, and the crying had stopped. But if a foot thumped upstairs, I froze. I dared not try another word. I felt, if I lose myself in my writing, and another thump comes, it will be excruciating. My good idea will vanish. While writing, I was continually reaching for and just barely seizing things being thrown to me. If a thump happened just when I was about to catch a thought, it would sail into the irretrievable beyond. So I sat suspended, waiting for a thump. It benefits my neighbor nothing to take my writing, I thought, and it costs me everything, my whole life, my mind, my creativity—everything. How *dare* she make my writing worth so little!

Similarly my sister-in-law and a friend's mother who happened to be in town and innumerable close friends haunted me. This one had said many pissy things at dinner; that other demanded too much. "Call soon," a friend said, and I had to call right away. If I suspected someone was angry at me—and my newly confrontational behavior seemed practically designed to provoke anger—I must force that anger into the open. I couldn't bear for anything to happen soon. It must happen *now*, so that it could be done with, and then I could immerse myself in my book with a feeling of safety.

All the danger I felt between me and the unwritten book was being forced out into the world, where I could contend with it.

"You are looking for tyrants," my friend Carole said.

I found them everywhere.

I noticed the tiny but constant ways I compromised myself. These used to be invisible, like paper cuts. Now the least artificial compliance on my part cost too much. It was as if a friend asked, "May I drink just a little bit of your blood? Just an eighth of a cup?" I could not sacrifice any part of myself for the sake of false harmony.

Faced with the extreme devaluation of my work which I projected out into the world, I at last had to be my work's champion, or the work would not exist. My voracious, devouring sister, whom I had grown up accommodating, had been unleashed. She was in me, and still punishing me now, twenty years later, for wanting to put my book out in the world because in the perpetually frozen era of our childhood it threatened her. How did it threaten her? It incited her envy. It was something entirely my own, an independent source of pleasure that seemed to enlarge me, and to make her more ordinary, more likely to be left behind. In response I felt furious. Rage was everywhere.

My landlady, a high-strung woman with chopped dyed-white hair, sawed and slammed under my floorboards every afternoon for a week. That week I could not write even in the mornings because the anticipation of her intrusion called up an answering rage in me so strong the red veins in my eyes seemed to have swollen and I could not see the computer screen. When the land-lady left, the red drained to my cheeks; they blazed with embar-rassment. And then the old depression overtook me, the tears and sense of futility. I felt like the internal air shaft of an apart-ment building. All around it plants thrive and children grow from nursery school to college. It, however, remains static, a mute column of dust, the trapped shadow just as it was when the building was first erected.

All this was occasioned by the moment of my success. Approval came for past accomplishments, but they did not match what was inside me, which was inchoate, scattered, obsessed, contradictory, a column of electrified dust—yet all that mattered. I had no faith that I could produce a book from it.

The everyday key which I was missing was of course the gleam of confidence: the sense that one's instinctive way is valu-able. It is the magic possession. Wanting it, I cluttered the win-dowsill with amethysts and blue origami cranes and inspirational quotes from Rilke, and a playing card that said EXTRA JOKER, which I had discovered face down on the street, and which my friend Mary said meant "a chance beyond chance. Why," she'd added, "it's even better than the Queen of Hearts!" A desperate hoard meant to remind me of what I had inside that was magical. Mute keys cluttering a windowsill.

Writing returned to me when I thought, Even my experience of this hollow feeling is valuable. Even this is real, and is my own. When I thought, My valuable book may begin even here.

I had entered therapy when I could not write. I discovered that I made sense even when I felt my worst. I did not have to strain. Wild riches were packed into even my bad feelings, like wild onion in dark grass. Here were long-abandoned clumps of meaning: sources of strength. This therapist took me at my word. She heard the truth—the meaningful voice speaking—in even the most frenetic emotions. She was skeptical of nothing in me. I had been accustomed to regarding my own thoughts as exaggerated, erratic, untrustworthy. Therapy started to cure me of this. Experiencing my own coherence brought my writing back to me.

A paradox happened. While I learned to give up my enchanting dream of the ideal book and accept the particular imperfect book that appeared, I felt as if I were building a stronger and stronger, or rather a bigger and bigger, inner self. I suppose this is because I accepted more of my split-off aspects. Parts of myself I'd estranged decades ago began to pulse with life, even the part of me that was my sister Anita. I tolerated more ambiguity in myself. My old way was to be like the Abraham who is abstract, glaze-eyed. What was ugly, anomalous, frightening, inconceivable—went into soft focus. All those tears that season I refused to write—didn't they keep the world a blur, a watercolor, dreamy and vague? They were like my friend's tears the day I sat on the hard, grimy kitchen floor—because of course I was my angry, tearful friend too—mournful and furious at the loss of the old dispensation, pining for the old way, the old closeness in which the phone didn't ring with a message of accusation, the old coherence during which I was solicitous, generous, nice. The world dissolved and dissolved in my tears, the season I sat bolt upright at my desk. I refused to be the ugly woman, the Wicked Witch who dissolves like an aspirin tablet. I refused to disintegrate into the various greedy, unseemly parts of myself by writing my book. Instead, I made the world drench and drain away. That was my protest. I was like my friend who wept because she couldn't stand to be the person who'd been hurtful and greedy. I wanted only to be beautiful and loved. I could not write until I could risk appearing ugly. Tears are the last resort of the dream. After the flood, a new spangled coherence emerges whose emblem is the rainbow, a whole spectrum. Writing this new, riskier way, I felt more substantial, more solid in the world, more real.

To surrender takes faith, and first of all one must have faith *in something* to leap. Abraham had faith in God, the Bushmen have faith in their religious passage and in the strength of the community to receive them back. Writers need faith that a kingdom of significance stands within. Faith is also the key to the kingdom. Experience teaches it. It is learned through the body and the spirit, not the mind, which is why advice helps so little. One must allow oneself an education of experience.

Silence departed when I embraced fragrant imperfection, the roses of the bush I discovered all overgrown in my yard. It had been an indeterminate tangled heap all through the first dank autumn we lived here, a prostrate sodden mass that winter. I assumed we had a yard of weeds. Only at the beginning of June did I notice the first blossom, a blush white. Soon there were dollops of cream all over the bush, each one plush as a satin cushion, the petals dusted with powder and turning a bruised translucent blue if held. I rarely touched them, though, merely watched them open more each day.

They opened past reason. They budded and bloomed and opened—more and more of them—until several branches sagged and at last lay on the ground, the big blush roses pressing open until their petals scattered in an opulent surge of scent. The rosebush taught me how winter rosebushes look, just as good ideas teach you to see other ideas that are not yet ripe, and to trust in them.

When I embraced imperfection, silence dissolved. The inner absolutist, the fanatic mistress of restraint who, suffering, defines herself through refusal, at last departed, or rather receded into me, which is of course where she'd come from in the first place. She had finally disclosed what was at her core: a hunger for faith.

GLITTERING ICONS, LUSH ORCHARDS: ON SUCCESS

I USED TO SHARE AN APARTMENT WITH A SKINNY, red-haired actress and a dancer with vast, honey-colored eyes who was continually rinsing her tights in the kitchen sink. The dancer's boyfriend was an actor. He didn't act. He had decided to play leading-man parts, and so was embarked on the expensive, time-consuming project of getting all his teeth capped. It was estimated that it would take two years to finish the dental work. In the meantime he watched TV.

He was a tall man whose body was fixed in an agreeable slouch. He always kept one hand slung in his pocket as if from gentlemanly modesty, or the desire to hold something in reserve. He draped his frame along the doorpost or curled into the corner of a room, a blond, wan, long-boned person in manila chinos and wheat-tone shirts, so very innocuous in his manner that one easily forgot he was there, and spoke as if to a room of girls. I suppose he thought his teeth would change all that.

His girlfriend took three or four dance classes a day. She strode to the studio chewing carrots and celery sticks, and marched home with chocolate bars in her hands. One day she saw an advertisement. Disney Studios was coming to Boston. She scribbled down the time and place, and intently practiced her routine. On the day of the audition she cut her blond hair into pigtails, wrote that she was nineteen, and sailed across the stage.

Out of several hundred, she was re-auditioned and eventually selected to be a dancer in Disney World, where she would not be allowed to curse, chew gum, neck with her boyfriend anywhere in public view, or reveal her true age, which was twenty-six. Of course, her boyfriend did not want her to take the job, which meant moving to Florida, and he pleaded with her to stay.

"If I go," she said, "I might be discovered. If I stay, it might take years to get an opportunity like this again." She went.

In those years we were all possessed of the idea that we might be discovered. It was as if we were unknown continents, genetic fugitives, galaxies spinning just beyond reach of the current telescopes, and we were waiting for the advance in technology that would establish us. The red-haired actress was at her theater every night, a place so small and makeshift, if you slammed the bathroom door the set collapsed. She played Curly's wife in *Of Mice and Men*, Laura in *The Glass Menagerie*, Maggie in *Cat on a Hot Tin Roof*, Lady Macbeth, and Golde in *Fiddler on the Roof*. She seldom woke before noon. She emerged down the corridor clutching her jade silk robe to her waist with a hand as shocking white as a plant root. For the first two hours she was awake, she was enraged. If you stepped into the kitchen, she snapped the pages of her magazine so hard they ripped. Then she stared into the alley until you left. If she was home in an evening, she was often drunk, and affectionate. She had few relatives, fewer friends.

She meant to go to New York when the time was right. She wanted to go when she could step right into a decent part. New York was too full of waitress actresses, Xerox-shop actresses—she would go when she was unassailably excellent, when she could audition and be hired just about on the spot. In the meantime, she seemed to adore this life of jerry-rigged sets and pasteboard tiaras, of morning touchiness and spare evenings being stewed— it all smacked of something she'd read in a book or seen in a movie when she was a child, one of those black-and-white movies where women are "kids" or "mice" or "hoofers" or "troupers," where the show is opening in Wappingers Falls day after tomorrow, and the leading lady just broke her leg. I remember the first time I saw such a movie. "That girl will fill in for the star. She'll be a smash," said my friend Amanda's mother, pointing to the screen.

"How did you know? Did you see it before?" I asked later.

"Oh, it always works like that."

What is surprising now is that there was ever a time one *didn't* know that that girl would fill in and be a smash, that the leading lady was frankly destined to break her leg. Most of us knew the formula for this kind of movie by the time we were thirteen, and now watch with a sort of nostalgic fondness, as if viewing a species of kitsch.

And yet, despite our awareness of the clichés, perhaps even strengthened by it, certain stories still exert a fateful glamour. The overnight success. Or the success after years of thankless anonymity. Or the failed writer, the failed actor. Or the man who remarks with a laugh (two men actually said this to me), "I went off to write the Great American Novel," and is now a fatigued editor, or fatigued professor—older and wiser, watering the cactus on his windowsill, pouring himself a stiff drink, speaking in a voice laced with a certain knowing bitterness, like George in *Who's Afraid of Virginia Woolf?* or the Michael Caine character in *Educating Rita*, their grandiosity turned to rage, their hopes turned to self-mockery, as if compelled to punish themselves for having dared aspire and thus at least, in this oblique way, to preserve their marvelous dreams.

What do we mean by success? What do we expect it to look like and feel like? Where shall we find the holy chalice, the elusive unicorn, the rose in its tangle of briers, the doe that's leaped over the hills? I saw the Holy Grail with my own two eyes. It was in the coastal town of Valencia, toward the south of Spain. Indirection brought us there. We were bound for Granada, to walk through the Moorish gardens. That was the great goal of our trip. We wanted to see the place where overblown roses swelled still further in the static heat, and where invisible waters trickled in secret conduits, imparting a sensation of coolness and of motion—and inducing, we found, a mild synesthesia, a confusion of sensation, so that after a long while in these gardens one surrendered to the suggestion that one was in fact far away, in a cool theater perhaps, watching oneself in a hot Arabian garden, entranced.

Arab artists "love the feeling of being lost," as Anaïs Nin said. "It has been interpreted as a desire to reproduce the infinite." Prohibited from representing sacred images directly, Arab artists used intricate repeated patterns to convey a sense of dislocation, of unearthly dizzying release, echoes upon echoes with mysterious subtle variations, curving garden pathways where you are sure you stood not five minutes before, although certain details seem altogether unfamiliar—are they new? are you just seeing what you did not notice earlier?—a gorgeous baffling of the mind that is in itself a gateway, a sensation of pathways that is in itself a gateway to a place long coveted yet close.

We wanted to walk in the Moorish gardens, and to bring home a trophy: a photo of ourselves there. This was the sole request my husband's father had made. He did not want anything from our travels but this, evidence of us in one of the wonders of the world—although when my husband placed the photo in his hand, his father glanced and kept talking, so that Paul placed the photo in his hand again, and yet again, and still his father scarcely acknowledged it, so that at last I said, "This is the photo you wanted."

"Uh-huh," he said, nodding irritably. "Well, as I was saying . . . "

He preferred his own stories just then to those of other people. Like many, he cherished his desire, because it was his, far more than someone else's satisfying it. The photo instantly became an emblem of disappointment to all of us, although I recall how earnestly Paul and I posed ourselves in that place whose power originates in the fact that depictions of the human form—of the entire material world—were disallowed there.

But the railroad would go to Granada only by means of Madrid, which was entirely out of our way and added eleven hours to the trip. So we decided to take the straight route along the coast, by bus. The train left us in Valencia, where the oranges were large but withered in the dusty heat, and where the sea shone far off with the dullness of steel. In the afternoon we wandered into a busy plaza in the old town. A man soaked Spanish baguettes in the public fountain then flopped them to the pavement, where they shattered and were instantly set upon by a long narrow oval of birds, like iron filings quivering around a magnetic bar. Pigeons moaned amid the cracked statuary of the cathedral, waddling back into alcoves beneath the stone saints. Inside, the corridor was murky, lit by lofty remote grilled windows. I turned a corner, peered into a case, and saw beside a modest wineglass a dusty index card typed "Holy Grail." Could it be? I consulted *Michelin*. Yes! It documented a "small purple agate cup, said to be the Holy Grail . . . The cup, according to legend, was brought to Spain in the 4C."

It was a little wineglass about three inches high with a wide purple lip and twin handles, so surprisingly unextraordinary looking—so in fact not actually beautiful (was it too coated with dust?) that it resembled the sort of little ornate object you'd expect to turn up on a cluttered card table at a flea market among random silver spoons and Pepsi glasses, and which you might pick up and glance at idly, then set back in its place.

I stared at the Holy Grail for several minutes. I hoped what was unique about it, what compelled men to abandon their homes and go through long treks and battles for it, would somehow be suggested in its appearance, but after a while I found I'd drifted, and was soon transfixed by the sight of an ancient human arm. The arm was five hundred years old and was not mentioned in *Michelin*. It too was a sacred relic, having been attached at one time to the living body of a man revered as a saint. It had flattened somewhat over the centuries, and was now a browned, leathery, flaky object refined into a sort of translucence. It began below the elbow and ended above the wrist, an unarticulated length of human body that looked both spooky and poignant behind its wall of glass, something not permitted to go into the earth, something whose death was simply refused, something held on to for a long, long time for any last blessing it might bestow.

Outside the sun shone brilliantly. It was wonderful to step into the fresh air. The plaza flickered with pigeons that strutted and pooled by the dozens, then sailed up in clattering waves. The air itself seemed to have been folded, and dyed gray and white and black, and set in motion.

"Look," my husband said.

A plump woman in a dark cotton dress squatted amidst a flock, her arms extended. Pigeons settled all over her. One or two strolled on her head, and a bunch stood on her arms, and a few even attempted to balance themselves on her breasts. She smiled, beaming—doves are associated with the Holy Spirit— and then, in an overflow of love, she turned her face and kissed a pigeon perched on her shoulder. She looked as radiant as a low-born woman who has just discovered she is a queen. Riches were strewn all over her.

We expect when we are successes we will be changed. We will be different from who we are now. We will live more intensely when we are successful, and our joys will be magnified, and our frustrations and sadnesses fewer and more meaningful because set in the context of our more significant lives—as if fame itself, or whatever we mean by success, establishes a force field within which everything counts, everything matters, simply because it has happened to us. When we are successful, then we will have reason to love our lives.

What do we imagine our published book will bring us? In part it is a trophy we want. Not entirely, of course, for we want all the pleasures of the writing, every single one of them, and we want all the pleasures of knowing that someone else may read our words and savor a story that once existed only in our heads—and yet in part there is a yearning for a trophy. But a trophy of what?

"We should find out the meaning of our effort before we attain something," Shunryu Suzuki says. "It is not after enlightenment that we find its true meaning. The trying to do something in itself is enlightenment."

What do I imagine it would be to hold my own novel, published, in my hand? What blessings do I imagine it—the physical object—to bestow? I cannot say. I can say, though, what it is to hold the book of someone else. When I hold Amy Tan's book in my hand, or Louise Erdrich's book, or the books of Mona Simpson, Alice Hoffman, Kaye Gibbons, almost any young woman publishing good novels today (how much more deeply we are touched by the success of a person of the same sex! Is every woman an alter ego? Our unconscious says "yes"), I imagine how happy these women were immersed at their desks, their ample stories unfolding within their minds, beneath their pens.

I imagine that they felt confident while writing, or rather, since when writing at one's best one is oblivious to oneself, that they delivered themselves over to their stories with great delight, and that their stories did not fail them. They went on journeys. They shut their eyes and before them rose up thickets of characters, and they wrote down exactly what each one said and wore and did, and I imagine it gave them happiness to put on the paper that someone named Alice, for instance, wore a hand-stitched green loden coat with birch toggles smooth as ivory, or that Claire, who knew six languages, three of them no longer spoken, and who kept her hair in a heavy yellow braid thick as a man's arm, spit in her cousin's tea before impassively carrying it out to him on a lacquer tray.

How marvelous these writers must feel! If you could see their faces while they wrote, I was sure you would see a half-smile of involvement and unaware contentment—it was the echo of this I saw when I gazed at the pictures of them on their books. Their photos were so familiar they were iconic. I saw in them a certain poise and a satisfaction that if intensified in the least would be smugness, although it was not smugness, and a look almost of triumph. Of course, this is projection; I am writing about what one sees—what I see—when viewing success.

What I saw were women in beautiful, even extravagant scarves or earrings or shawls or elaborate hats, women who could allow something theatrical into their appearance because now they could certainly carry it off, women who seemed remote, fixed, aloof, far from mess, unconfused. They seemed to say, "I wrote this, and this is just the beginning. I have many more books in me. There is a place within me I can touch, and when I touch it I feel writing. What I have within me, the world considers beautiful. You may covet it, but it belongs to me. But here it is. It speaks for itself."

This is what another's book in my hand said to me. And so I assumed that for me to write a book I would need to feel like that. Sometimes in fact I did feel like that. Sometimes a euphoric feeling of potentiality possessed me. This happened while writing, when a scene opened up like a meadow after a journey through dark woods. It happened at times while I was thinking of places I would write about, thinking how rich in texture a certain chapter I planned to write could be.

And yet, just as swiftly, a feeling of desolation overcame me, a feeling that all the pages I'd ever written amounted to scraps and shards, empty shells—like the pumpkin-seed shells that lie all over the bottom of railroad compartments in Spain. The travelers leave, the lights flicker and go out, and the dark compartment remains empty and used in the deserted station, the crackly discarded shells of *pepitas* all over the bottom of it.

I know because one evening a girlfriend and I stayed on board after everyone left. (This was when I was nineteen, years before I returned with my husband.) I had lost a contact lens. In the dark, as we touched the shells lightly with our fingers, everything felt like a lens. We could hardly tell. We squatted, patting the refuse with its dusty, almost silky sides, hoping for a gleam from the station that would show the lens amid the gray and black shards—and the whole time I pleaded with my girlfriend to leave with me, leave with me, but she would not. She loved me, and wanted me to have my lens. I didn't want her to go through so much trouble.

"Forget it," I said. "It's hopeless."

"But I want to find it," she said, her hands sorting through darkness.

Fingers tingling from all that delicate, futile patting, we at last gave up, and emerged into the vaulted, grimy atrium lit by distant yellow bulbs. This was the end of our trip. We were fatigued. It was late. The vast space around us opened forebodingly. Good-bye, good-bye, we murmured, as if just wishing each other good-night before sleep.

On the train and then on the bus, the faces of the few passengers looked more like strangers than I had ever seen strangers look. In my apartment, beneath the harsh bathroom light—I started. There it was! My contact lens glinted in the mirror, clinging to my shirt. Nevertheless, in my dreams that morning (it was daybreak), my companion and I were still searching on the stopped train, prolonging the moment because to leave was certainly to choose blindness and lack of beauty, while to stay was at least to choose this searching if perhaps futile companionship.

Is every woman our alter ego? Our unconscious says yes. We are all three women I have named: the iconic woman whose photo is on the flyleaf, the cherished companion who perseveres with oneself, and the dumbfounded narrator—the I—who has lost her clear vision and squats in darkness, panicked, stroking the ground.

"Only the living presence of the eternal images can lend the human psyche a dignity that makes it morally possible for a man to stand by his own soul, and be convinced that it is worth his while to persevere with himself," writes Carl Jung. "Only then will he realize that the conflict is in *him*, that the discord and tribulation are his riches, which should not be squandered by attacking others; and that if fate should exact a debt from him in the form of guilt, it is a debt to himself."

The iconic woman with her serene face, her possession of the kingdom you covet—she is installed above you like a stone saint. She is an emblem of what you think you must become to be happy with yourself. But her essential trait is that she is an image, a photo on a book: she is paper and ink; she is wood and glass; she is not alive, she is not the living person who wrote this book—you have no idea who that is; even if you have read a dozen interviews and articles about her, all you have are a dozen interviews and articles, you have a papier-mâché figure built out of newsprint—and if you offer her baskets of admiration and envy, if you bring her beakers full of your very lifeblood, it will make no difference. What she has will remain hers and will not become your own.

That is her function. That is why you have created her. She is Other, and because she is Other you have attributed to her all the virtues and satisfactions you yourself do not possess. Cynthia Ozick once wrote about a prolific writer: "I am not like him because I do not own the permission to write freely, and zealously, and at will, and however I damn please; and abundantly; and always. There is this difference between the prolific and the nonprolific: the prolific have arrogated to themselves the permission to write."

Arrogate: To claim or seize *without justification*.

If, while writing, you must always be proving that you write well, the writing will suffer. If you must be establishing something about yourself that is not yet established, you will tart up the writing in some way or other, and do pyrotechnics rather than the particular work of fiction, which, because it is committedly local—about these specific characters, this particular place—runs the risk of seeming inconsequential. One must arrogate the permission to write. One must shrug before icons. Siddhartha slipped from the palace in rags so he could know the real lives of the people outside his gate. His father, who wanted to protect him from suffering, had concocted a beautiful kingdom of artifice to beguile him. In this kingdom he never saw anybody grow old or poor. All romances continued happily. Everyone seemed to have just what they wanted. It was a Disney World with him as the sole audience. Age and sadness happened off-stage. Siddhartha gave up the world of enchanting appearances. And when he set his hand on an actual piece of local ground, he attained enlightenment.

Our icon fills a function; it does real work for us. What is the work of the icon? It says heaven on earth exists, although it is possessed by another. It says the kingdom of appearances is actual truth, although someone else reigns there, savoring the world's joy. All that remains is for you to go on a crusade. Prize happiness from the hands of the Other; reclaim the grail that has slipped into another's grasp. Forsake the rocky ground of your own orchard with its big withering oranges and crumbling huts, and journey far from yourself. Far from yourself is where happiness lies. Far from yourself is what's beautiful and good. When you have at last arrived far, far from yourself, then you will dwell in a land of milk and honey. You will be a real writer. You will wake up knowing you are a writer and go to sleep knowing it. You will trust that you have gold within you, like the top caste in Plato's mythic republic.

The icon knows she has gold within her. "Write the way I do," she suggests. "Write in my voice, write about my topics, live where I live, speak the way I speak. Forsake your own way. After all, I am where you want to be."

The icon shows that what you dream of is possible. And yet she keeps it just that—a dream.

And the friend who perseveres—what does she say? She sees your blindness and wants you to recover. She sees your dis-orientation, your suspicion of what is most good in yourself, your inability to sort dross from gold, wealth from anxious poverty.

"I know it's here somewhere," she says, touching shards, searching for the lens.

Yet how can she ever find it? You never ceased to possess it. It fell, but it did not fall away from you.

My friend walked into a room where students discussed writing their doctoral dissertations. This was on the board:

    A. It's great! Just what the world needed.
    B. It's garbage. I can't believe I wasted all my time writing
        this worthless piece of . . .
    C. It's okay. Not bad, really. Actually, I kind of like it.

Between A and B is an easy fall. B comes to us with the terrifying air of truth. Between B and C—now, *that's* the key. For that one must persevere with oneself.

The companion teaches perseverance. She provides an example. She trusts that what seems hollow can be valuable, that gems may hide in cinder-gray junk. Even someone you respect and admire is not above searching through debris. Emerson writes, "A man should learn to detect and watch that gleam that flashes across his mind from within, more than the lustre of the firmament of bards and sages. Yet he dismisses without notice his own thought, because it is his. In every work of genius we recognize our own rejected thoughts; they come back to us with a certain alienated majesty." Amid the refuse, amid the parts of ourselves that we refuse, the most precious insights glint.

The best examples must be left behind, at last. Even Emerson, even the beloved friend. One disembarks alone in the blurry city. It is like losing one contact lens. Out of one eye, the streets look snipped with a scissors. Out of the other, they are watery, dissolving shapes whose borders are forever giving way, like 3-D Rorschachs. One eye is reason and the other emotion. One eye is what you know makes sense and the other is how you feel things to be. Should you have been let loose in this condition? Shouldn't you have received just a bit more education? Heart banging, you depart alone into the tangled interior regions with no guarantee at all—it seems the unlikeliest thing!—that all this will end in clarity, in focused vision, in something you yourself discover that suits your eyes exactly.

One woman is the goal, the other the goad. One figure is the competitor, the other the companion. One figure is who you wish to be, the other is who loves you as you are. One figure is before you, the other is at your side. Thronged thus, we each advance.

My dreams came true one day. I was discovered. It was just as I had always imagined it would be.

It was a dull hot morning late in August. Sweat seemed to hang in the air. The scene on my desk went nowhere. I sighed and began to reread the page. The telephone rang, and I snatched it before the machine could pick up, glad for the interruption.

"Hello," a woman's voice said. "May I speak with Bonita Friedman?"

The name used by the student loan agencies.

"This is Bonita Friedman," I said with abrupt decisiveness. I try to sound like time is money when I talk with them.

The woman told me her name. It sounded familiar, like something I'd read on a slip of paper sometime. "I'm calling from *The New York Times Book Review*," she said. "We're going to run your piece."

My face pounded so hard my cheeks tingled. "Oh, I'm pleased," I said, scarcely able to breathe, but thinking I ought to act self-possessed.

"Payment will be a thousand dollars."

An enormous magic number! A jackpot! "That sounds good," I said. But in a moment, as soon as she was done explaining the editorial process (I shouldn't expect to hear from them for quite a while; a week or so before they were going to print it, the copy editor would go over all suggested changes with me), I exclaimed, "Oh, I'm so excited! I can feel the blood beating all through my body! I'm just absolutely thrilled!"

"I don't see why you should be," she replied drolly. "It was well written."

Well written! As if for years I hadn't been writing prose exactly as good! As if for years I hadn't received rejection after rejection from literary magazines! The remark dizzied me.

As soon as we hung up, I dialed my husband, away on a business trip. While the receptionist located him, I glared hard at the tabletop, as if I wanted to impress it with the absolute truth of what just happened.

"Guess what!?" I yelled when I heard his voice. "*The Times* is going to run my piece!"

"You're kidding!" he yelled back. "That's phenomenal!"

"I know!" I shouted. "The editor just called!" And I loudly told him all about it—as if to imprint the truth of it into the very air—from the scene going nowhere to the "I don't see why."

After that, I called my mother at work, and then my father at work, called them with the feeling that at last I could announce the thrilling news that I had made good, that their hard years of raising me had paid off, that the gamble was worth it, that they had every right to feel proud of me now. These were strange calls to make. Until I had this news to deliver I hadn't realized how urgently I had wanted to deliver it. I called everyone I could think of, until I was turning the pages of my little telephone book, looking for another name.

Then I set to my heels. In my stiff leather shoes and jeans, I flung out the door into the stifling air and ran as fast as I could around the block.

"It's too hot, honey," a man called genially as I flew past.

I just smiled. I was delighted to have a good reason not to return to the scene on my desk, which, since I had been struggling with it all morning, was still on my mind. My life has changed, I thought. I've turned the corner.

It was a spectacular day and a spectacular week.

The rejection slip came toward the end of the month. Below the *New York Times* heraldic gothic masthead—a form rejection, without so much as an editor's initials. "We regret to inform you . . . " and my heart seized in my chest. Here was my manuscript back! My life hadn't changed! It was a mistake, a horrible, regrettable mistake! Feeling foolish, but to make double-sure, I picked up the phone.

"Send it back immediately! We don't have a copy!" the editor said. "Oh dear, I gave it to the secretary to input into the computer, and she returned it to you by accident."

It all seemed strangely haphazard for a moment. As if one submitted to a machine that spewed out hundreds and hundreds of rejections, and which occasionally jammed, doling out an acceptance, or a rejection where there should have been an acceptance—and who knows whether to pick up the phone and question it, or just to put one's faith in the face-value of what arrives at your door.

I took my indelible orange Magic Marker and wrote in a chain all around the rejection slip "HA! HA! HA! HA!" as if in revenge on the smug definitiveness of rejection slips in general, or as if in a sort of voodoo punishment of this particular rejection slip. HA! HA! HA! HA!—as if to demean the object and thus forever defeat the power of rejection over me.

And yet one day a month after this I opened my door and found a rejection—a real rejection—of a short story. Then an essay came back. I reeled. It was okay when the story came back. Maybe I didn't know how to write stories yet; my big acceptance had been an essay. When a journal returned an essay, though, I lay down on the couch. My cheeks burned, my throat burned, I felt so weak I could not stand. I wished the couch would swallow me, would just roll over me and erase me. I was insupportable the way an argument is insupportable. Whatever was sometimes wrong with my work was still wrong with it. Some bad thing leaked out of me while I worked, and I didn't know it. It was identical in my eyes to what was actually good. How could I go on when I sent out junk as if it were treasure, and the rare treasure as carelessly as junk?

I had a giant blind spot that ran through the center of me. It was from here that writing came. The spot was like the dangerous space big enough for a car to emerge from, which I walked through one night. I was arguing with my father about why he should glance over his shoulder before merging left.

"You can't rely on mirrors," I said, although he'd been doing just that for forty-five years.

He looked dubious.

I stepped out and circled the car. "Can you see me?" I called. "Check your mirrors." I paced forward and back.

"Not a bit!" he said. "Can't see you at all"—although I think I was more surprised than he, walking through my father's blind spot.

I was all my own blind spot, it seemed. I didn't know what would come out of me. The *Times* acceptance had given me the feeling this had changed. But how could this be? A phone doesn't ring and make you someone else. If someone discovers you, is it the same as you discovering yourself?

Many of my students are waiting for a sign. They want to know that now it's time for them to commit to their work. They want to write something up that very afternoon and have an expert say, "This is brilliant. You must give up your full-time job and devote yourself to your writing," or else, "This is brilliant. Let's send it to *The New Yorker* immediately! They'll print it, and your life will be changed!"

Because they are waiting, they do not write as hard as they can. And because they assume someday writing will feel different from the way it does now, they squander many true gifts.

They assume, as I did, that when they are successes the risks will be different, the blind spot will be gone, and when they go all-out in their writing, when they rush gloriously past all the known signposts, that even then they will not feel insecure. When they are successes, they will feel entitled to take time from their families, and they will know their work's importance. When they are successes, they assume, the goodness of their work will rise from the page and wash over them with undeniable persuasiveness, rinsing away the writer's own doubts. When they are successes they will deserve to be happy.

Is that it? Is that what is so very dangerous about our idea of success? For there *is* something dangerous about it. Our idea of success makes some people rush desperately and others dawdle painfully or sit in an absolute seizure of writer's block.

The phrase "young hopefuls" suggests what's wrong. The phrase "he is a nobody" or "he's really somebody" suggests it too. It is the Cinderella idea of transformation from ash-heap to palace, from goose to swan, from a girl in a shopping mall in Boise to Miss America beneath a glittering crown on national TV.

What's wrong with our idea of success is that it detracts from everyday life. It distracts us from the beauty our work already reveals. It makes us feel somehow that all this is "before," that when we are somehow established or recognized, all this will be left behind. It puts the focus in the wrong place.

I live in dread that the story I am currently writing resembles those that have been rejected. They are bad, I think. When I recognize emerging on the page a rhythm similar to the rhythm of one of these "bad" stories, or when I recognize a character that turned up in one of them, I am appalled. I want to cross it out. I want to put away from me forever everything associated with those "bad" stories because frankly I do not really understand what was wrong with them. Something was probably wrong; one must be realistic enough to admit it. Yet it feels as if my new writing comes from the exact same place.

The idea of success divides us; it cleaves us. It makes us want to name some great piece of us "bad" and the rest, the undiscovered part perhaps, as "good." And it is the "good" that will save us, that will transform us, that will deliver to us the confidence of those we admire as well as their material achievement. The "bad"—that old familiar impulsive, groping, gooey, fixated, feverish self that keeps turning up on the page; the self that is "too much"—can't be dispatched with fast enough.

Yet our finest writing will certainly come from what is unregenerate in ourselves. It will come from the part that is obdurate, unbanishable, immune to education, springing up like grass. It will come from who we already are and how we already write. To love our lives right now—that is the transformative success. To see what is already beautiful—that is the astonishing strength.

Outside the cathedral holding ancient relics in Valencia, a woman kissed pigeons. She saw these birds as symbols of God. Gray and white and black as discarded shells, these were creatures I'd been taught to think of as "filthy." They *seemed* filthy, in fact, with their staring orange eyes and patchy feathers. But now, while I looked, they turned into doves. Of course they always were doves, or rather, of course doves always really were a type of pigeon. But I never really believed it until this woman showed me her belief. Her kiss transformed ugliness to beauty.

So it was like a fairy tale after all. It was the old story: what is loved reveals its loveliness. Here she squatted, radiant, smiling, enrobed in life, in a dozen pairs of folded wings, in a dozen pairs of pearl gray and, as I looked, yes, even lavender, even royal purple wings—a woman in an ordinary black cotton dress who smiled as if she knew she was the luckiest person on earth, swathed in blessing.